GETTING GOD TO TALK BACK

Secrets of the Lord's Prayer

GIL STIEGLITZ

PTLB
PRINCIPLES
TO LIVE BY
LIFE IS RELATIONSHIPS

Principles To Live By Publishing
www.ptlb.com

Getting God to Talk Back: Secrets of the Lord's Prayer

Published by Principles To Live By Publishing, Roseville, CA, 95661. All rights reserved. For more information about this book and the author, visit www.ptlb.com.

Cover design by John Chase
Copyedited by Jennifer Edwards (www.jedwardsediting.net)
Book design by Kelly Stuber

ISBN: 978-0-9968855-5-3

RELIGION/Christian Life/Prayer
RELIGION/Christian Ministry/Discipleship
RELIGION/Prayerbooks/Christian

All Scripture verses are from the New American Standard Bible unless otherwise indicated.
New American Standard Bible: 1995 update. 1995 La Habra, CA: The Lockman Foundation.
Printed in the United States of America

DEDICATION

This book is dedicated to:

God the Father, God the Son, and God the Holy Spirit,

who have invited me (and everyone else) into this

dynamic, loving, wisdom-filled, blessed, and empowered
relationship with them

through the secrets in this prayer.

Thank you. It is amazing!

CONTENTS

HOW TO USE THIS BOOK

IN MY MIND, I SEE THE LORD'S PRAYER AS A SERIES OF PULL-DOWN MENUS TO ACCESS DURING MY time of prayer. Each menu is a possible discussion that God and I will have about a particular subject. I slowly pray through the various topics as God highlights and directs me to spend more time on one topic more than others. Then I pull down the menu for that particular topic, and God and I have this rousing discussion about what's going on in my life and the people I care about regarding that topic, and how it fits in with my day, week, month, or year.

To help guide your time of prayer, I've outlined the "menus" that I use. These lists or pull-down menus allow your mind to linger over biblical ideas and allow God to whisper to you what He wants to discuss or explore with you further. Each of these concepts are explained in much more depth in the designated chapter; this outline is meant to help give you a picture for how a structured time with God might look as you pray through the Lord's Prayer. You can focus on one area or all, as you feel led.

Our Father in heaven. (Ch. 2)

What fathers feel and do for their children >
Fathers allow their children to approach them.
Fathers want their children to run up to them and hug them.
Fathers want to hear all about their children's day and adventures.
Fathers want to see their children do well and succeed.
Fathers look to provide every advantage they can for their children without spoiling them.
Fathers show the look of love in their face when their children approach them.
Fathers want to educate their children about why they didn't succeed the last time.
Fathers want their children to ask them for help.
Fathers comfort their children when they are hurt or confused.
Fathers protect their children from many, but not all, difficulties.
Fathers want their children to be wise, not just smart.
Fathers take the time to teach and train their children to survive and thrive in the world.

Hallowed be Your Name. (Ch. 3)

Which aspect of Your wonder do you want me to focus on? >

Is it your Omniscience? Pause and let Him respond.
Is it your Omnipotence? Pause and let Him respond.
Is it your Omnipresence? Pause and let Him respond.
Is it your Unchanging Nature (immutability)? Pause and let Him respond.
Is it your Holiness? Pause and let Him respond.
Is it your Goodness (love, mercy, grace, and blessings)? Pause and let Him respond.
Is it your Faithfulness? Pause and let Him respond.
Is it your Long Suffering? Pause and let Him respond.
Is it your Sovereignty? Pause and let Him respond.

Which aspect of Your Name do you want me to focus on? >

See "Praying through the Titles and Names of God" in the Appendixes.

Your kingdom come. Your will be done, on earth as it is in heaven. (Ch. 4)

Fruit of the Spirit—Which one of the Fruits of the Spirit do I need to focus on for tomorrow? >

Is it Love?
Is it Joy?
Is it Peace?
Is it Patience?
Is it Kindness?
Is it Gentleness?
Is it Goodness?
Is it Faithfulness?
Is it Self-Control?

Beatitudes—Which one of the character qualities of Christ do I need to focus on for tomorrow? >

Poor in spirit (humble, grateful, teachable, self-assured)
Mournful (grieving pain, losses, wounds, and guilt)
Meek (power under control, impulse control, thoughtful requests, and wise adaptations)
Hungry and thirsty for righteousness (desperate desire to bring about what is right)
∨

∧
Merciful (not demanding every ounce of vengeance)
Pure in heart (positive, pure, and edifying thought life)
Peacemaker (reconciliatory, bringing harmony, order, and calm everywhere I go)
Persecuted for righteousness and for Christ

Ten Commandments—Which of the Ten Commandments do I need to focus on for kingdom benefit tomorrow? >

You shall have no other gods before Me
You shall not make for yourselves any graven images
You shall not take the name of the Lord your God in vain
Remember the Sabbath Day to keep it holy
Honor your Father and your Mother
You shall not murder
You shall not commit adultery
You shall not steal
You shall not bear false witness against your neighbor
You shall not covet anything that belongs to your neighbor

The Ten Events—What events do I need to prepare for the future coming kingdom? >
Wars and Rumors of Wars
The Great Falling Away
The Great Tribulation
The Antichrist
The Abomination of Desolations
The Rapture of Believers
The Return of Christ
Resurrection of the Dead
The Millennium
Judgment Day
The New Heavens and the New Earth

Give us this day our daily bread. (Ch. 5)

There is much more to talk with God about than just bread. He wants us to talk with Him about all of our needs in every arena of our life. Spend time going over these areas with God. Ask Him for things that we really do need and also things that we want. Pray through each one of the ten basic relationships to see which one God wants you to focus on, then ask Him what basic need is needed in order to make that relationship healthy or whole. I have given an example below.

Ten Basic Relationships >

God – *What spiritual, mental, emotional, physical, or relational need is needed to make your relationship with God healthy or whole?*
Personal Development
Marriage / Romance
Family
Work
Finances
Church
Friends
Society
Enemies

Basic Needs >

Spiritual
Mental
Emotional
Physical
Relational

And forgive us our debts, as we have also forgiven our debtors. (Ch. 6)

I regularly have to go over this list of issues that allows me to have a pure heart. If I allow the injustice and problems that will happen to grow into bitterness and hatred, then my life will be diminished significantly.

Steps of Forgiveness	>
Confession of our own sins	
Forgiveness and release of bitterness	
Forgiving ourselves	
Setting goals so we don't stay stuck	
Letting God love us and flow through us in new ways	
Bringing peace: embracing harmony, order, and calm	

Lead us not into temptation. (Ch. 7)

Pray through each of the ten basic relationships, asking God, "How am I being tested, tried, or tempted in my relationship with _____?"

Ten Basic Relationships >
God – spiritual and moral life
Self/Personal development - mental, spiritual, emotional, and physical
Marriage / Romance – spouse, girlfriend/boyfriend, or single status
Family – immediate and extended
Work - work, career, businesses, bosses, colleagues, and subordinates
Finances - your money, generosity, trying not to have it become a god or idol.
Church - church and/or support system
Friends – close friends, neighbors, acquaintances
Society - your community, region, and nation
Enemies - those who oppose you or are your rivals

But deliver us from evil. (Ch. 8)

I find that God wants me to regularly become aware of how evil is stalking me. We need to talk about how we can win against evil plans and strategies. We do not want to be blindsided, and we won't be if we have discussions with God about the nature and types of evil and how they are circling our lives.

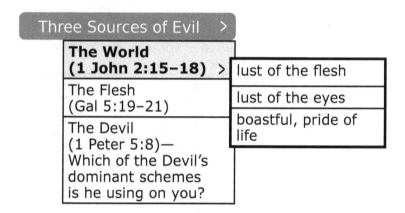

Three Sources of Evil >	
The World (1 John 2:15–18) >	lust of the flesh
	lust of the eyes
The Flesh (Gal 5:19–21)	boastful, pride of life
The Devil (1 Peter 5:8)— Which of the Devil's dominant schemes is he using on you?	

Three Sources of Evil >	immorality
The World (1 John 2:15–18)	impurity
	sensuality
The Flesh (Gal 5:19–21) >	idolatry
	sorcery
The Devil (1 Peter 5:8)— Which of the Devil's dominant schemes is he using on you?	enmities
	strife
	jealousy
	outbursts of anger
	disputes
	dissensions
	factions
	envying
	drunkenness
	carousing

Three Sources of Evil >	
The World (1 John 2:15–18)	
The Flesh (Gal 5:19–21)	Tempter
	Opposition
The Devil (1 Peter 5:8)— Which of the Devil's dominant schemes is he using on you? >	Slander, Lies, Rumors
	Fear
	Anger
	Spiritual Power
	Perversion
	Pride

God has provided equipment to shield us from attacks by the Devil. We need to look at the Armor of God passage and have a discussion with God about these vital protection pieces. (Eph 6:10–18)

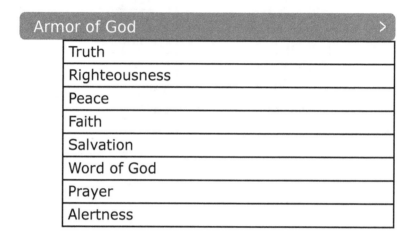

Armor of God >
Truth
Righteousness
Peace
Faith
Salvation
Word of God
Prayer
Alertness

For Yours is the kingdom and the power and the glory forever. Amen. (Conclusion)

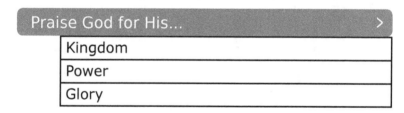

Praise God for His... >
Kingdom
Power
Glory

INTRODUCTION

S EVERAL WEEKS AGO, I HAD THE OPPORTUNITY
TO SPEAK AT THE CHURCH WHERE I GREW UP. I
love this church and here's why. When I was growing up, it
was a normal, and what I considered, "boring" church, until
the leaders did a few unique things. The first thing they did
was to hire a renegade youth pastor to breathe life into the
youth group. He was anything but a typical youth pastor,
because he did not believe being a youth pastor meant he
should be a party planner. Instead, he actually believed
that God was alive and his goal was to inject the living God
into every one of the kids in the group. Every time I would
see him he would either ask me or the other kids, "What is
God doing in your life?" or "Did you have your quiet time
today?" He asked any number of other questions just to see
how active God was in our lives. We had to be on our toes!
The impact this man had on the students was tremendous.
Why? Because of these questions—they automatically
invited God into the conversation. And you can bet that we
always had great stuff to talk about in group, as God did
some pretty amazing things through us.

Most churches are wonderful social clubs where
people gather to strengthen friendships and honor God for
the deeds He did long ago. But it's rare that a church tells
of the miracles that have just happened, the stories that are
occurring around us and through us every day. A typical

Christian is a good person who serves others when they get the chance to and hopes that God blesses them. But few expect God to show up every week and deliver miracles in and through their lives. They think miracles either don't happen today or they are for some other, more "spiritual" person. I'm here to tell you that I don't believe the above description of church or of the Christian life is what should be taking place. Remember, I was trained by a man of God who refused to believe that the living God wanted to stay distant from His people. God is alive and active and wants to do things in your life in ways that you cannot possibly understand. He wants to ignite hope in your career, breathe life into your marriage, initiate blessings in ways you can't even imagine, all by redirecting you toward things that glorify Him.

Though most of us have heard of the "Lord's Prayer," we have been vaccinated against its power. I believe that Jesus' prayer for the disciples is actually a series of invitations to ignite and experience God talking back to us. If God were to talk back, what would that be like? God speaks to our soul, our spirit, not through our ears. His is the inner voice that whispers to us to love, rejoice, be at peace, do good. His responses "appear" in our minds to move forward in advancing His kingdom, let forgiveness happen, receive His blessings, grow past the mistakes of the past. All of this is a part of the dialogue with God that He wants to have with us. Yes, we will hear other "voices" in our minds—voices of temptation, of selfishness, anger, and hate, but we know that they are not from God and are not to be followed. Stop paying attention to those voices and begin a dialogue with God Almighty that will change your perspective and your life. It is so worth it. There is a new generation coming up, who really want God to show Himself in strong, tangible ways towards them and around them. It is through this mechanism of prayer that God moves in incredible ways. Listen for His voice.

To those who want to experience the tremendous blessings God has for them, this book will show how to ignite God's incredible power in their lives. The Lord's Prayer has become rote to many of us. We have been taught that it is for reciting, not really for praying and expecting answers. Let me show you the hidden powers within this incredible prayer that believers in Jesus Christ have full access to—right now, today. If you really seek to understand the principles Jesus taught, then put these simple prayer exercises into practice. You will find your life becoming a conduit of miracles—today and every day.

Let's begin by looking at the Lord's Prayer in Matthew 6:9-13 (NASB):

"Pray then in this way;

Our Father who is in heaven,

Hallowed be your name,

Your kingdom come,

Your will be done, on earth as it is in heaven.

Give us this day our daily bread.

And forgive us our debts, as we also have forgiven our debtors.

And do not lead us into temptation,

But deliver us from evil.

For Yours is the kingdom and the power and the glory forever. Amen."

The book is made up of nine chapters and a conclusion, each one representing just one of the sentences in the prayer. Besides instruction on how to begin and end in prayer, the Lord's Prayer consists of really seven different topics to engage God about that relate to your life. These topics open up crucial areas of life where you need God's help and where He wants to help you. Together, we will explore the seven topics and I will provide a number of simple prayer exercises for each one to draw God's active power out into your life in this area. This prayer, taught to us by Jesus Himself, introduces these as areas where we can expect God to do miracles or advance blessings into our life if we will ask Him.

In essence, there are nine "dialogues" we can have with God for His powerful touch on our lives:

Phrase:	Dialogues to have with God:
Our Father who is in heaven	For God to become the Father to us He longs to be. God wants to change our approach to Him from distant to familial. We must get this switch of perspective.
Hallowed be Your name	For God's Spirit to swallow us up in His presence.

Phrase:	Dialogues to have with God:
Your kingdom come	For God to make us perceive His kingdom activities, to be kingdom-minded now and for His future coming.
Your will be done, on earth as it is in heaven	For God's perspective to become kingdom agents, delivering goodness to others and representing heaven on earth.
Give us this day our daily bread	For God's provision, daily and special, to allow us to become the kingdom agents He wants us to be.
And forgive us our debts, as we also have forgiven our debtors	For God to deal with our sins against others and others' sins against us so our connection with God will be incredibly strong.
And do not lead us into temptation	For God to give us the chance to avoid some trials, testing, and temptations. This is incredibly beneficial.
But deliver us from evil	For God to keep us from evil plans against us; to help us be prepared and delivered, lest we become sidetracked, at best, and destroyed, at worst.

Phrase:	Dialogues to have with God:
For Yours is the kingdom the power and the glory forever. Amen.	For God to help us embrace the idea that life is all about God and His purposes and plans and not about us.

When Jesus says that He will teach us to pray, He is not saying that He will give us a more effective way to submit our desires to the heavenly warehouse. To Jesus, prayer is your relationship with God; a dialogue with God, not a list of requests. When Jesus says that He will teach them to pray, He is offering them the secrets to an incredible relationship with God. He tells us the topics and types of interactions that a human must have with God Almighty if they want an Abram-type of relationship with God. Remember that he (Abram) was called the "friend of God." (Jas 2:23) It is close, intimate relationship with God that Jesus is offering through these prayer secrets based upon His life, death, and resurrection.

Many times, when Christians pray (including myself), it reminds me of when I take my dog for a walk. I think that my dog understands me when I ask if she (Roxie) wants to go on a walk. Whenever we are on the walk, she always wants to go in directions that I am not going. She pulls ahead faster than I want to go; she chokes herself, because she is working so hard to go in directions I won't allow her to go; at times, she gets distracted as she stops to smell some disgusting thing that is fascinating to her. If I let her off the leash, then she dashes after this smell or that noise and endangers herself by chasing after something meaningless. She has a completely different agenda than I do. I want to walk through the park to get to a particular place, while she wants to respond to anything in her environment that interests her in the moment.

In the same way, when God invites us to pray, He has an agenda. He has things He wants to talk about and things He wants to do to and through us. His list does include things we want and need because He cares for us, but that is not all of what He wants to interact about with us in prayer. When we pray, God is inviting us into the most important chamber in all the universe—the control center, the holy of holies. He is inviting us into His presence to talk about something and to bless our lives in a personal way. We can be an agent for Him, which is His desire for us.

But often, when we start to pray, all we can think about is all the stuff we want, what would make our life happier, and the complaints about why He is not acting faster to fix our problems or the problems of those we love. We treat prayer as if it were a requisition request from headquarters. *"If He really knew what He (God) was doing, He would give me what I need,"* we think to ourselves. Or, *"If He really loves me, then He would grant what I have requested."* We don't understand why God doesn't do what we want when we want—*because we're not kingdom-minded.*

I am amazed at the number of people who have just given up on prayer because they don't get the answers they want. God wants to talk to us but about different things than we want to talk about. Yes, He will meet our legitimate needs, but there are many other things to talk about that will make a huge difference in our lives. Even in the early church, many Christians had this problem. We see it on the pages of Scripture, as James wrote:

You do not have because you do not ask. You ask and do not receive, because you ask with wrong motives, so that you may spend it on your pleasures. (James 4:2, 3)

Join with me to learn how to pray powerful prayers that will inject unimaginable blessings and miracles into your life, which will really give you something to talk about at church, with friends, at work, and everywhere. God is alive and wants to do miracles in and through your life, now and every day.

1.

GOD, TEACH ME HOW TO PRAY!

"This, then, is how you should pray:" (Matt 6:9a)

THE LORD'S PRAYER IS ONE OF THE MOST COMMON SCRIPTURES IN THE WORLD. Thousands of people have memorized this prayer and have no idea that they are reciting from memory one of the most powerful keys to intimacy with God and access to His power. There are secrets in this prayer that will unlock a whole new depth to your spiritual life, hidden keys that will ignite the miraculous here and now. Jesus teaches in this prayer a whole new way of approaching God and living for Him. We want to experience the unimaginable blessings in our lives, and this is where it all begins.

In ancient times, to speak of prayer was to talk about your relationship with God, the Creator. Prayer encompassed all the things you did to interact with Him. These were called spiritual exercises or spiritual disciplines. The more that you did these spiritual exercises, the more religious you were. "Prayer" was the one word that described all of these spiritual exercises that both demonstrated your faith and connected you to God. That is why it was very important to the disciples to understand what Jesus thought about prayer (spiritual exercises).

What we call the Lord's Prayer was clearly given as instruction for a believer's relationship with God (prayer) on numerous occasions (with slight differences) to the various groups of disciples throughout Jesus' ministry. This is evidenced by its inclusion in the Sermon on the Mount in Matthew 6, a parable on prayer in Luke 18, and as the answer to a question posed by the disciples in Luke 11. By far, the more interesting context is in Luke 11. This is how the instructional time in prayer begins in verse 1.

> *"It happened that while Jesus was praying in a certain place after He had finished, one of His disciples said to Him, 'Lord, teach us to pray just as John also taught his disciples.'"*

Here, Jesus was praying and the disciples were watching Him converse with God the Father and God the Holy Spirit. They had witnessed something tremendous and were privileged to see such an incredible sight! Imagine if you had been able to watch and listen to Jesus pray. Wouldn't you have been amazed, humbled, and delighted all at the same time? You would have hung on every word you heard. Wouldn't you have wanted Jesus to guide you into that kind of prayer? What topics is He covering? Which spiritual exercises is He using? How is He responding to God's interaction? Watching the Son of God and the perfect Son of Man interact with God the Father and God the Holy Spirit makes your mouth drop open and your mind swirl. It forces you to ask Jesus to teach you what is important for that kind of relationship with God. Jesus' kind of prayer was real and intimate and meaningful.

The disciples witnessed a dialogue between three people in a relationship—between Jesus (the perfect man), God the Father, and God the Holy Spirit. He was showing His disciples then, and now us today, that to relate to God is so far above us and beyond us.

The ancient world was full of ritualistic-types of interaction with God, as illustrated in Matthew 6:5-8.

> *"When you pray, you are not to be like the hypocrites; for they love to stand and pray in the synagogues and on the street corners so that they may be seen by men. Truly I say to you, they have their reward in full. But you, when you pray, go into your inner room, close your door and pray to your Father who is in secret, and your Father who sees what is done in secret will reward you. "And when you are praying, do not use meaningless repetition as the Gentiles do, for they suppose that they will be heard for their many words. So, do not be like them; for your Father knows what you need before you ask Him."*

When the disciples were asking Jesus to teach them to pray, they were not asking for Him to tell them what to say or what lists to recite. They were not asking Him to make better rituals. Rather, they had just seen Jesus do something completely different than they had ever seen or thought to do with God before. In Jesus' prayer, they noticed a "realness" and an interactive communication between Him and God (the Father and the Spirit) that they were not familiar with. Imagine if you had just heard someone pray to God in the most authentic, transparent, and intimate way. You would have just witnessed a man who got answers back from God, conversing with Him in a real relationship. The disciples could hardly wait until Jesus finished before they asked Him to teach them how to pray. "How do we do what you just did?" "We want to relate to God like that!" "We want to have a relationship with God like you have!"

What is interesting is that Jesus did not rebuke them for wanting what He had. He went on to tell them how to adjust their prayer life so that they could enter into a level of relationship and receive answers to prayer that they had never experienced before. They wanted to know about what Jesus had just done so they, too, could have a real relationship with God that they did not have at the present time. When the disciples were asking Jesus to teach them to pray, what they really wanted was what Jesus had—the kind of relationship He had with the Father.

Is this even possible? Yes. Sometimes we are so aware of the fact that Jesus is God Himself that we fail to realize that He also lived His life on this earth as a man. He was the second Adam, the perfect man who was sent to redeem all of humanity by bearing their sins. (Rom 5) It is only when Jesus prays in John 17 that He speaks so clearly of His deity and the connection that He has within the Trinity. Because believers in Jesus also have the Holy Spirit within them, they, too, can relate with God today in the same way He did as a man way back then. (John 14:26; Acts 2:38; Rom 5:5)

Prayer Exercises:

In the religious world of the time of Jesus, everyone realized that a relationship with God was practiced through particular, often formalized, spiritual disciplines, and/or exercises. But Jesus wants His followers to have an intimate and non-formalized relationship with God, just as He has with God the Father and God the Spirit. He tells His followers on repeated occasions to practice different spiritual exercises in their conversation with God than was expected at that time.

Today, let's take a look at three of the major instructions on prayer that are recorded in the pages of Scripture, as taught by Jesus. Spend time reading these sections over, and let Jesus guide you to a completely different type of prayer with God the Father, God the Son, and God the Holy Spirit. You will be surprised and delighted if you just let the words Jesus says speak for themselves.

Matthew 6:5–15

"When you pray, you are not to be like the hypocrites; for they love to stand and pray in the synagogues and on the street corners so that they may be seen by men. Truly I say to you, they have their reward in full. "But you, when you pray, go into your inner room, close your door and pray to your Father who is in secret, and your Father who sees what is done in secret will reward you. "And when you are praying, do not use meaningless repetition as the Gentiles do, for they suppose that they will be heard for their many words. "So do not be like them; for your Father knows what you need before you ask

Him. "Pray, then, in this way: 'Our Father who is in heaven, Hallowed be Your name. 'Your kingdom come. Your will be done, On earth as it is in heaven. 'Give us this day our daily bread. 'And forgive us our debts, as we also have forgiven our debtors. 'And do not lead us into temptation, but deliver us from evil. For Yours is the kingdom and the power and the glory forever. Amen.' "For if you forgive others for their transgressions, your heavenly Father will also forgive you. "But if you do not forgive others, then your Father will not forgive your transgressions."

Luke 11:1-13

It happened that while Jesus was praying in a certain place, after He had finished, one of His disciples said to Him, "Lord, teach us to pray just as John also taught his disciples." And He said to them, "When you pray, say: 'Father, hallowed be Your name. Your kingdom come. 'Give us each day our daily bread. 'And forgive us our sins, For we ourselves also forgive everyone who is indebted to us. And lead us not into temptation.'" Then He said to them, "Suppose one of you has a friend, and goes to him at midnight and says to him, 'Friend, lend me three loaves; for a friend of mine has come to me from a journey, and I have nothing to set before him'; and from inside he answers and says, 'Do not bother me; the door has already been shut and my children and I are in bed; I cannot get up and give you anything.' "I tell you, even though he will not get up and give him anything because he is his friend, yet because of his persistence he will get up and give him as much as he needs. "So I say to you, ask, and it will be given to you; seek, and you will find; knock, and it will be opened to you. "For everyone who asks, receives; and he who seeks, finds; and to him who knocks, it will be opened. "Now suppose one of you fathers is asked by his son for a fish; he will not give him a snake instead of a fish, will he? "Or if he is asked for an egg, he will not give him a scorpion, will he? "If you then, being evil, know how to give good gifts to your children, how much more will your heavenly Father give the Holy Spirit to those who ask Him?"

Luke 18:1–8

Now He was telling them a parable to show that at all times they ought to pray and not to lose heart, saying, "In a certain city there was a judge who did not fear God and did not respect man. "There was a widow in that city, and she kept coming to him, saying, 'Give me legal protection from my opponent.' "For a while he was unwilling; but afterward he said to himself, 'Even though I do not fear God nor respect man, yet because this widow bothers me, I will give her legal protection, otherwise by continually coming she will wear me out.'" And the Lord said, "Hear what the unrighteous judge said; now, will not God bring about justice for His elect who cry to Him day and night, and will He delay long over them? "I tell you that He will bring about justice for them quickly. However, when the Son of Man comes, will He find faith on the earth?"

Prayer is really a way of talking about the kind of relationship you have with God. It is not about making lists and standing or kneeling in a particular way. Write down what you learned from these passages about what your relationship with God could be like from Jesus' teaching in these sections. Write down what you also learned about prayer.

1.

2.

3.

4.

5.

6.

7.

8.

9.

10.

In the next chapter, we will delve into more about the kind of relationship God wants to have with us as our Father. Get ready to hear one of the most shocking revelations about prayer from Jesus himself!

2.

FATHER, I WANT TO BE CLOSE TO YOU!

"Our Father who is in heaven," (Matt 6:9b)

I N THE PREVIOUS CHAPTER, WE LEARNED THAT PRAYER IS REALLY A WAY OF TALKING ABOUT THE kind of relationship you have with God. It is not about making lists and standing or kneeling in a particular way. We are not bound by these types of rules. Jesus wants His followers to have an intimate and non-formalized relationship with God, just like the one He has with God the Father and God the Spirit. This chapter will uncover the basis for His thinking.

At the very beginning of the Lord's Prayer, Jesus makes one of the most shocking declarations in the whole of His instruction on prayer with these words, *"Our Father who is in heaven."* He addressed God in such a way that established intimacy with God as our Father. This interacting with God on a *familial* basis, instead of a formalized Creator-to-creature basis, or All-Powerful-King-to-subject basis, was shocking to the disciples, to say the least. This was no ordinary relationship based on formality and ritual; this was real, intimate relationship with the Creator Himself! This is the way to begin an effective, powerful prayer.

During Jesus' earthly ministry, He set the example for every follower about how to have an intimate, non-formalized relationship with God. He modeled perfect relationship that one can experience between man, God the Father, and God the Spirit. The disciples observed first hand Jesus' intimacy, connection, and closeness with God—that is what Jesus was offering in this opening phrase. This was not formal and distant, as was typical in the way the Israelites understood and addressed God the Father. Notice how the Psalmist addressed God in Psalm 104:1-4.

> *Bless the LORD, O my soul! O LORD my God, You are very great; You are clothed with splendor and majesty, Covering Yourself with light as with a cloak, Stretching out heaven like a tent curtain. He lays the beams of His upper chambers in the waters; He makes the clouds His chariot; He walks upon the wings of the wind; He makes the winds His messengers, flaming fire His ministers.*

There are hundreds of prayers like this one in Scripture, where the creature is submissively asking the almighty powerful God for help and wisdom. That is *not* how Jesus says to go about interacting with God. Instead, His message is this: "If you are intrigued by my relationship with God, then start from a different place in approaching Him." In other words, if you start from a formal, distant place, you can't get to the kind of relationship you desire to have with God—the kind of relationship where blessings and connection happen to you and through you.

Look at Matthew 6:6-8, the instruction Jesus gave the disciples before He gave them the keys to effective prayer:

> *"But you, when you pray, go into your inner room, close your door and pray to your **Father** who is in secret, and your **Father** who sees what is done in secret will reward you. And when you are praying, do not use meaningless repetition as the Gentiles do, for they suppose that they will be heard for their many words. So do not be like them; for your **Father** knows what you need before you ask Him."*

Now we know theologically that our connection to God as Father is only through the work of Jesus Christ in His life, death, and resurrection for our sins. This opening phrase is based upon the work that Jesus would do. One could say that the "Our Father" at the beginning of this prayer was praying in Jesus' name, because that is what this relational connection with God was all about. Jesus is inviting us into the family. He is inviting us past the screens, sins, and servants into the presence of God Almighty on a completely different basis—the basis of our connection to Jesus. Essentially, Jesus gave us the ability to say to God, "Jesus said we could come in and talk with you."

A story that comes to mind to illustrate this point is the story of a soldier during the Civil War. He had a medical emergency back home and was going to be granted leave, but he had to see the President. He not able to get in to see the President and so was told that he would not be granted leave because it was not authorized. He went to a nearby park and sat on a bench, buried his face in his hands and wept. A little boy saw him and approached, and asked the soldier what was wrong. After hearing the soldier's story about needing to see the President and how it couldn't happen, the little boy just said, "Follow me." The soldier got up and followed, though he did not know who the little boy was. They approached the White House through a back way and every guard just kept waving the boy through with the soldier in tow. The little boy breezed right into the White House, past the guards, and into a meeting of the President and his cabinet. The President stopped and joyfully greeted Tad, his son. "Who have you brought with you?" the President asked. "This is a soldier, who desperately needs to see you," said the boy. The soldier got to explain his circumstances and the President signed his petition for leave.

This is the way that it is with Jesus. Because of who He is and what He has done, we get to walk past all the normal protocol and formality and talk to God as one of the family. *This changes everything.*

For one thing, this moves the intimacy factor forward much more quickly because sons and daughters can approach a king, a business leader, or a celebrity more directly than practically any other person. They are able to get past all the guards, assistants, and protocol relating to the real person. When you start the conversation with God from the position of a Father-son or Father-daughter, then the relationship can get very close from that point. This was scandalous for the disciples to hear. They were being taught something entirely new to them—that is, to move forward with the assumption that they had a Father-son or Father-daughter relationship with God at that moment. Their faith in God was enough to allow them to begin interacting with God in that intimate way. Faith was the only basis, not anything else they had done themselves. Think about it.

Fathers allow their children to approach them.

Fathers want their children to run up to them and hug them.

Fathers want to hear all about their children's day and adventures.

Fathers want to see their children do well and succeed.

Fathers try to provide every advantage they can for their children without spoiling them.

Fathers show the look of love in their face when their children approach them.

Fathers want to educate their children about why they didn't succeed the last time.

Fathers want their children to ask them for help.

Fathers comfort their children when they are hurt or confused.

Fathers protect their children from many, but not all, difficulties.

Fathers want their children to be wise, not just smart.

Fathers take the time to teach and train their children to survive and thrive in the world.

This is what true intimacy with God the Father can look like—isn't that amazing? God wants to do all of these things for you and with you, but you will only get to this level of intimacy if you begin with this related-like, familial posture of believing faith. We need and God wants for us to share deeply with Him our thoughts, feelings, and troubles, asking Him for help and insight. He wants intimacy with us. He wants to do miracles through us and to bless us.

Remember, this is what the disciples heard Jesus doing with God the Father and God the Spirit. He was here on earth as the perfect man living His life completely dependent upon the direction and guidance of the Father and the Spirit. He did not relate to God as the Son of God but as the Son of Man. He was our perfect example of humanity. He was the Lamb of God, who took away the sin of the world. He was climbing into the lap of the Father regularly asking for guidance for the next day, the next hour, and sometimes, the next moment. He was waiting (in his humanity) for instruction and wisdom for each step in His earthly journey. It was this intimacy, dependence, guidance, and authentic relationship that caught the disciples' attention. They wanted what Jesus had with God.

Jesus said intimacy with the Father begins from where you start, with God as your perfect Father. It is astounding that Jesus invites us into this familial relationship based upon work He was *yet* to do on the cross. The disciples were children of God by faith. Jesus said He would fix it so that everything would be okay. They believed and trusted him. You can too.

Now, if you had a selfish or evil father, you may not have any good reference points to what a real father is supposed to be like. But that is why I included the descriptors for what a good father does for his children above. I had a great father growing up, and it has been easier for me to transfer all of my earthly father's traits and care to my heavenly Father. But even if you didn't have a great earthly father, you can approach God as your Father and He will be there for you. You don't have to repair your relationship with your earthly father in order to have a great relationship with your heavenly Father. You can go straight to God and treat Him in the above ways, realizing He is different than your earthly father. God will always come through. He cares deeply for you.

There is a great deal of literature in our present day about "the father wound." This is the wound that exists between many children and their father, because the father-figure was emotionally, physically, or mentally unavailable to the kids. Our present culture is extremely selfish and self-focused, which has allowed or caused many men to abandon their families and create a huge hole in the lives of their children. Growing up without a father leaves a void that can be very difficult to overcome. We need the men who father children to step up and really be there for their kids. We need to hold up the unique and critical role that fathers play in the lives of their children. We can elevate that role by approaching God as our heavenly Father and building the type of relationship with God that we all need.

God Is Near

Another secret hidden in this phrase "Our Father, who is in heaven" is about the nearness of God. By telling His disciples to pray to the Father who is in heaven, Jesus was telling His disciples that God was right next to them. His omnipresence is being emphasized in this phrase. God dwells in eternity, which surrounds and exists throughout our three-dimensional existence. The Greek phrase *tou ouranou*, translated heaven(s), means to the modern reader distance, center of the universe, or distant space. To the Jewish disciples, however, it meant the opposite. It meant the nearness of God. To say that God was in the heavens means that He is all around us. Jesus is saying "Our Father, who is near." The other day, as I began praying with this realization that God is near, that He was right next to me in the room that I was praying in, it changed my tone; in fact, it changed the entire conversation! I was talking with God as though He was sitting right next to me, which He was. Instead of turning in a bureaucratic way to a distant super being, I had a dialogue with my heavenly Father who was right in the room and wanted to listen. The back-and-forth conversation went much deeper than most request-based prayers I have heard. *Enjoy the closeness of God* is what Jesus is saying. He loves you, wants your best, and is closer than you can imagine.

The term *tou oranou* could mean the atmosphere, space, or where God dwells. In our modern world, we have emphasized the space aspect, while the Old and New Testament emphasized the atmosphere or dimensionality where God dwelt. God spoke to Hagar from another dimension but pushed into the atmosphere around her to tell her about the well that would save her son. God spoke to Abraham from another dimension when He spared Isaac but through the atmosphere around Abraham. God was present surrounding the Mountain of God, Sinai. The Jews understood that God was all around them. He was able to be near them wherever they were and was so close as to know what they were thinking. (Psalm 139:1-11)

I have always enjoyed the story of the announcement of the birth of the Savior as the one angel proclaims the news and then a whole host of angels can't hold back and appear shouting the news. They were all there around the shepherds for some time. The angel appeared and rescued Peter from the jail; the angel did not have to come from a long-ways off.

When Jesus tells His disciples to pray to God as their Father who is in the heavens, He is telling them that God is very near—as near as the atmosphere around them. In classic, theological terms, God is omnipresent. But Jesus wants His disciples and followers to live in the light of the fact that God is all around them. I tend to think about God's nearness as God dwelling in some hyper-space or super-dimensional space above, beyond, or in our three-dimensional space. But in fact, He is right there, just not visible to us. However, He makes Himself known to us as we live in full view of His presence all the time. Reach out and talk to God who is right there. That is what Jesus is saying. There are times when I just want to walk through the dimensional walls and go home to be with Him (just like Enoch), but until that time comes, I know that He is right here with me.

Prayer Exercises:

I realize that some of you need to begin repairing the relationship with your earthly father but do not put off a great relationship with your heavenly Father just because your earthly father was selfish or evil. Pour out your heart to your heavenly Father. Do the work to finish the following sentences. As for me, I get into one of my two favorite chairs and have an actual conversation with God that goes something like this:

- Dad, I need to tell you about...

- Dad, I need to get your wisdom about...

- Dad, what do you think I should do about...

- Dad, I need to ask you to do some things for me...

- Dad, I hope you are not asking me to...

Think about these questions and really ponder them in your heart. Write down the answers to these questions.

When you begin your prayer time, imagine that God is right there next to you (which He is), like He is sitting in the chair across from you. Allow yourself to have a back-and-forth conversation like you would with a friend that you could physically see and touch. Remember, He really is there all around you.

Take your time with both of these and let yourself enjoy this process. It really is wonderful. Trust me!

In the next chapter, we will launch into the first of the several different dialogues that God says we can have with Him for His powerful touch on our lives. What does it mean to "hallow" God's name? Let's find out.

3.

GOD, SWALLOW ME UP IN YOUR PRESENCE!

"Hallowed be Your name." (Matt 6:9c)

IN THE PREVIOUS CHAPTER, WE LEARNED THAT WE CAN APPROACH GOD WITH FULL CONFIDENCE as His sons and daughters if we have faith in His Son, Jesus Christ. (Eph 3:12; 1 John 5:14, 15) We do not have any ordinary relationship based on formality and ritual; but because of Jesus we can have a real, intimate relationship with the Creator, Himself! (Heb 2:10, 11; 12:7-9) We now know that this is the way to begin the kind of prayer that will unleash unimaginable blessings and power in our lives.

Now we'll see the first of several dialogues that Jesus tells us we can have with God, which involves "hallowing" His name. Most of us don't recognize what Jesus is actually saying, because we are not familiar with the language of worship. Millions of people say this phrase "hallowed be Your name" every day and miss what Jesus is really asking

His followers to do here. He is not asking us to say the phrase "hallowed be Your Name." The word *hallowed* is the Greek word *hagiadzo*, which means to make sacred, to set apart, to revere. He is asking us to engage in adoration and holiness exercises that will elevate our thinking of God so that He will occupy the supreme place in our lives He deserves. Only when we embrace all that God is will we let Him be Lord of our lives.

Jesus is telling us how to have an intimate yet powerful relationship with God (in this model prayer), like He does as the Son of Man (a human on this planet). This kind of relationship with God requires that we practice our faith by practicing certain spiritual exercises—it's not going to happen all on its own; we actually have to practice. Jesus lays out those particular exercises that He wants His followers to be regularly engaged with in order to connect with God. Now, let me add that Jesus is coming from the assumption that all that God has done and will do through Him will make this connection with humans possible (Creation, Incarnation, Propitiation, Resurrection, Redemption, Ascension, and the giving of the Holy Spirit, among a myriad of other actions). But if we, as Jesus followers, do not participate in the relationship that God the Father, the Son, and the Holy Spirit have won for us, there will be no relationship because there is no faith (John 3:16; 3:36). We have to do our part in this two-sided relationship, which is why Jesus teaches us how to pray—to engage in a deep, meaningful interaction. Yes, God will exalt His majesty in answer to this request, but we must participate by focusing on God and allowing ourselves to lift Him higher in our thoughts.

What is interesting is that "hallowed be Your name" isn't a petition for God but a petition for us! We are supposed to *hallow* God's name. In other words, we are asking God to tell us (remind us) how wonderful He is. Jesus has just blown the minds of the disciples by telling them to approach their time with God from the point of view of seeing God as their personal heavenly Father, with a familial tone and posture as sons and daughters. This intimate, personal, and emotional relationship could, over time, cause His followers to "humanize" God in a way that is inappropriate. We're not to be "chummy" with God— He's still God! So, to keep that from happening, Jesus tells us that after we approach God as our Father, we are to allow Him to magnify our understanding of Himself to the level of His transcendence. We are essentially asking God to help us realize, in a way we can handle, His transcendence— His wonder and magnitude and power and grace. Jesus tells us to spend some time at the beginning of each prayer exalting God in order to reorient ourselves to Him in this world.

There are four aspects of hallowing God's name: 1) a focus on God alone; 2) our willing participation; 3) an ushering into God's presence; and 4) interaction with God about Himself. Let's take a look at each of these areas in more detail. My hope is that these instructions and ideas for worship will help you experience God like you have never experienced Him before.

From Self-Focus to God-Focus

So much of this world tries to distract us from thoughts of God, doesn't it?

The distractions come from the world, our flesh, and the Devil, who all want us to be completely occupied with this world, our life, our emotions, our wants, and our needs. Have you noticed that so much of our thoughts consist of our own plans? We constantly think about what we are going to do with this issue, or what we think about what someone said, or how we are going to react to what that family member did, or what we want in regards to something, and so on. It's all about us! Our own natural inclinations are self-focused. But Jesus knows that we must rise above that and catch a glimpse of God. We need to see our life from God's perspective and that will only happen if we remind ourselves regularly of how magnificent He is. If we are going to experience the power of God moving in and through our lives, then we must break through this natural, self-focused perspective and "see" God.

The answer to this break-through is, you got it— hallowing God's Name, which is done through adoration and exaltation (worship) of our great God. Keep in mind this is not just for when we go to church weekly (worshipping God weekly is very important, see Hebrews 10:25), but also daily, as Jesus instructs in Matthew 6:11. You can do this during private devotions and in moments throughout the day. Hallowing God's name doesn't have to be formal or take long amounts of time. How we speak to another person could hallow God's name. How we think at a particular moment can hallow God's name. Whether we execute God's plan or our plan can hallow God's name. We are separating God and ourselves into a "place" where

He is king, we are not, and His plan is our primary desire. The idea is growing an intimate relationship between you and God. The Almighty wants a relationship with you. He is your heavenly Father, and He wants this relationship between you and He to be primary.

God is not going to hit us with a holy zap so that we always have a great relationship with Him and never need to pray again. Though I do hope I am hit with lots of spiritual experiences and electric times with God, I will still need prayer and worship as a regular part of my life to keep the connection close. Our modern world wants instant and permanent fixes that require no ongoing maintenance. But we must *daily* take the time to take our focus off of ourselves and put it on God. This focus shift will help us with our prayer life immensely.

Just the other day, I was awakened in the middle of the night and could not go back to sleep. I was meditating on the Lord's Prayer, just saying the phrases over and over. The Lord whispered that I needed to practice the "hallowed be Your Name" phrase, so I began exalting God according to His attributes: His omniscience, His omnipotence, His omnipresence, His immutability, His holiness, His longsuffering, His goodness, His faithfulness, and His sovereignty. The more I thought and explored these ideas about the wonder of God, the more delightful my time with the Lord became. The more I allowed my mind to be overwhelmed with the Supremacy of God, the more I could see my life and my decisions correctly. This is what God wants us to do as we interact with Him—not just pray the words.

Next time you are awake in the middle of the night by your worries, pressures, or cares, practice hallowing God's name by thinking on one of His attributes. Start with the attributes God gives Himself in Exodus 34:6–7, one of my favorite passages:

> "*Then the Lord passed by in front of him and proclaimed, 'The Lord, the Lord God, **compassionate and gracious, slow to anger, and abounding in lovingkindness and truth;** who **keeps lovingkindness for thousands**, who **forgives iniquity, transgression and sin;** yet He will **by no means leave the guilty unpunished**, visiting the iniquity of fathers on the children and on the grandchildren to the third and fourth generations.'*"

Our Willing Participation

Praying the Lord's Prayer invites our participation. In Matthew 6:9, Jesus says "worship God" in the most interesting way. He essentially says, "Ask God to hallow His name." The idea here is to focus on God and be reminded that He is sufficient for all of your problems and difficulties.

If we are going to get the relationship with God that Jesus tells us about, we need to practice all the parts of this relational prayer. We need to spend time lifting up our ideas and thoughts of God until they are worthy of Him. That is why I often go through His attributes as I practice this element. We must participate in this relationship with Him or there will be no relationship. I have listed some of the attributes of God below, and you can find an explanation for each, plus some additional ones in the Appendix, "Exploring the Attributes of God."

Ask the Lord, *"Which aspect of the wonder that you are, Lord, do you want me to focus on?"*

- *Is it your Omniscience?* Pause and let Him respond.

- *Is it your Omnipotence?* Pause and let Him respond.

- *Is it your Omnipresence?* Pause and let Him respond.

- *Is it your Unchanging Nature (immutability)?* Pause and let Him respond.

- *Is it your Holiness?* Pause and let Him respond.

- *Is it your Goodness (love, mercy, grace, and blessings)?* Pause and let Him respond.

- *Is it your Faithfulness?* Pause and let Him respond.

- *Is it your Long Suffering?* Pause and let Him respond.

- *Is it your Sovereignty?* Pause and let Him respond.

Look at John 17 as Jesus practices this idea of "hallowing" God's name. In this priestly prayer, His focus is on the glory of God right before His crucifixion.

"Father, the hour has come; glorify Your Son, that the Son may glorify You, even as You gave Him authority over all flesh, that to all whom You have given Him, He may give eternal life. This is eternal life, that they may know You, the only true God, and Jesus Christ whom You have sent. I glorified You on the earth, having accomplished the work which You have given me to do. Now Father, glorify Me together with Yourself, with the glory which I had with You before the world was."

This magnificent prayer condenses the conversation of Jesus with God the Father as He, Jesus, agonized and interacted with God about His mission and the salvation of mankind. We know that this interaction in prayer took all night because of the various accounts in the gospels. But notice that the hallowing of God's name is clearly there in the beginning of this prayer time. It is not wooden; it is not a one-phrase request (hallowed be Your name), but it is an interaction about the glory of God being accomplished through what Jesus was doing and about to do—His participation in the redemption of mankind. There will be many times when our own participation is needed to bring about the things we ask for.

Ushering into God's Presence

Jesus is saying that we need to hallow God's name, to exalt Him in our life, so that we can literally be swallowed up in His presence. His presence will transcend the here and now and take us to a new place: an eternal place where His presence is manifest. If we connect with God deeply, the rest will work out.

Jesus communicates this when He interacts with God in John 17:3—

> "This is eternal life, that they may know You, the only true God, and Jesus Christ whom You have sent."

This passage reveals that knowing the Father, the only true God, and the Son, Jesus Christ, is eternal life. This is hallowing God's name—it is revering it, setting it apart, and acknowledging that He is first in your life. There is something wonderful and powerful that happens when God truly becomes first in our lives. When God's position becomes primary in our lives then the relationship begins to generate the intimacy, blessings, and power that Jesus is planning for His disciples.

Going back to the previous section, we know that worship allows us to change our focus from ourselves to God, since we know that too much of our lives is spent focused on what we think, what we want, our problems, our perspective, our solutions, and so on. Instead, we will learn to exercise our spiritual, mental, and emotional muscles by focusing completely on God—by lifting up His majesty, adoring Him, reminding ourselves how powerful and amazing He is.

This can be a very difficult thing to do. In fact, one of the most difficult things to do in our modern world is focus our minds on God. There are so many distractions and nonsense toys meant to capture our attention. It is time to put those aside and contemplate Him and Him alone. So how can we do that? How can we experience God's presence during our time of worship?

For me, there is no greater way to be ushered into the presence of God than by listening or singing great worship songs that exalt God. This may be what some of you do already. For some of you it will mean composing your own songs, writing, painting, or photographing something for each one of the names. The goal is to focus on God and exalt who He is and what He is all about. Reading a list of the names of God may remind you of how AWESOME He is, but the idea here is not that it is a set ritual or rote thing; instead, insert creativity into your regular time of relating to God—a time of reminding, reverencing, and repeating His wonder. After all, God is tremendously creative and created us to also be creative each in our own unique way. Perhaps that's why He created human beings with artistic talent and an eye for beauty, so that it would be used in worshipping Him.

Take time in your day to reposition God as the center of your world as the primary decider of your life. This exaltation of God into His rightful place is hallowing Him. Do not fall for our culture's idea of "following your heart" or doing "what feels right to us." God will work in and through our lives as we set Him apart to His rightful place in our life.

If you are like some and must sing to enter into His presence, then I would suggest you have a rich playlist of worship songs that allow you to contemplate the wonder and majesty of God in the musical style that fits you. Some have found that painting, dancing, or exercising to music while focusing on the majesty of God to be very powerful. Over 2,000 years of Christian history has shown Christians using visual, musical, intellectual, emotional, and physical arts to *hallow* the name of God in their minds. All of it is wonderful. All of these ways are important spiritual exercises to enter into the presence of God. Try some new creative ways to expose yourself to the biblical content of who God is and let His name be hallowed in your midst.

Interact with God about Himself

In his book, *Exposition of the Gospel According to Matthew*, William Hendricksen says,

"In ancient times, the name was not generally regarded as a mere appellation to distinguish one person from another, but often rather as an expression of the very nature of the person so indicated, or of his position, etc."[1]

1 Hendriksen, W., and Kistemaker, S. J. (1953-2001). *Exposition of the Gospel According to Matthew, Vol. 9.* (Grand Rapids: Baker Book House), 327.

In other words, a name was more than just a way to tell one person apart from another; one's name declared who that person was—what they were all about!

If the goal of Matthew 6:9 is to hallow God's name through worship, another way to do that beyond creative expression (music, painting, dancing, and so on) is to spend some time reflecting on the names of God. When was the last time you went through a list of the names of God and reflected on who He really is? If a person's name declares who that person is, then that means we can know more about God by what His names mean. This is a powerful exercise and you can really experience the wonder of God by practicing it. Allow the majesty, immensity, and wonder of God overwhelm you. If God highlights a particular name, then look up those verses and push into worshipping and adoring God through that name. He may want that aspect of Himself to be known more fully by you. This is His way of interacting with you.

I must say that I love this exercise—to just read the list of His names and contemplate the majesty of God. I look at the Scriptures where we find these aspects of God's being mentioned and remind myself when God has been those things for me.

I've created a partial list of God's names, which you can find in the Appendix, "Praying through the Titles and Names of God." You will want to read each one slowly and prayerfully. God will highlight one or two of His names because He is trying to tell you something you need to know about Him and your present situation. These are the titles and names of God, and He will typically allow one or two to stand out to you—His way of interacting with you. Begin praising God that He is this name. Think of when He has been that for you. Go back and remember the times when you have seen God work in these ways. Describe how you need God to be that for you in this present situation. Ask Him to come through in these ways.

You approach God on this intimate, familial basis by calling Him Father, but now is the time to constantly remind yourself how impressive and significant God is through the rehearsing of His names. If you would like a fuller treatment of the understanding of these names of God and the rich tapestry that they weave about who He is, then you may enjoy my book, *Touching the Face of God: a 40-day Journey of Worship.*

In the next chapter, we will get a good understanding about Jesus' desire for us to discuss with God how He wants to make the kingdom of God appear in our world through us via our actions. This is another dialogue we can have with God about how we will show the people of this world the reality of the next.

4.

GOD, HOW CAN I SERVE YOUR KINGDOM?

"Your kingdom come. Your will be done, on earth as it is in heaven." (Matt 6:10)

Isn't it incredible that we worship an approachable God who desires to be intimate with us? We worship a holy, set-apart God. That's what it means to "hallow" God's name. Jesus is asking us to approach God on a familial basis by calling Him "Father" and by focusing on His significance and magnificence, rather than our own.

This next aspect of the Lord's Prayer addresses God's kingdom. There have been lots of books written on the topic, describing its features, when it will come, how it will only be fully realized at the return of Jesus Christ, and so forth. We don't know when He will come back, but the kingdom is already here. (Matt 3:2) God wants to show others what it looks like in our world today, through us.

The early church was consumed with the kingdom of God as a practical experience in their lives. They lived with the conscious reality that Jesus could come back at any moment, but also that they were to be living under the rule and governance of God every day in every part of their lives. Jesus' admonition in Matthew 6:33, "Seek ye first the kingdom of God and His righteousness and all these things shall be added unto you," only makes sense if it means seek God's rule (His kingdom) over every part of your life and the righteous actions He wants you to do. Every Christian was to be a part of the kingdom (the rule of God) for that day in their world, hoping that day was the day Jesus arrived. Interacting with God (prayer) was about receiving His kingdom orders for that day until the day Jesus split the sky and returned physically. John Calvin writes, "They are mistaken who think the Kingdom of God means Heaven. It is rather the spiritual life, which is begun by faith in this world and daily increases according to the continual progress of faith."[2] God wants us to have a dialogue with Him about being in the kingdom and preparing for the kingdom.

As we pray for the physical return of Christ (1 Thess 4:13–17, Rev 19), we should discuss with God how He wants us to give people glimpses of His kingdom through our actions now (Rom 14:17, 18, Matt 6:33). Let's discuss both of these dialogues, beginning with God's present-day kingdom here on earth, then how we can prepare for the future glory of His return.

---

2 Calvin, John, *The Gospel according to Saint John.* Translated by T.H.L. Parker. (Grand Rapids: Eerdmans, 1959), 63.

Prayer for God's Present-Day Kingdom

This verse "Your kingdom come" is about Jesus telling us to ask God how He wants to make the kingdom of God appear in our world through us via our actions. When we submit to the rule of God in our lives something changes and God brings His power, grace, wisdom, and blessing to our lives. Listen to what Dallas Willard says about the kingdom of God in his classic book *The Divine Conspiracy,*

> "Now God's own kingdom, or rule, is the range of His effective will, where what He wants done is done. The person of God Himself and the action of His will are the organizing principles of His kingdom, but everything that obeys those principles, whether by nature or by choice, is within His kingdom."[3]

> "Accordingly, the kingdom of God is not essentially a social or political reality at all. Indeed, the social and political, along with the individual heart, is the only place in all of creation where the kingdom of God, or His effective will, is currently permitted to be absent."[4]

> "So, when Jesus directs us to pray 'Thy kingdom come,' He does not mean we should pray for it to come into existence. Rather we pray for it to take over at all points in the personal, social, and political order where it is now excluded; 'On earth as it is in heaven.' With this prayer, we are invoking it, as in faith, we are acting it, into the real world of our daily existence."[5]

---

3 Willard, Dallas, *The Divine Conspiracy: Rediscoverying Our Hidden Life in God.* (San Francisco: HarperSanFrancisco, 1998), 25.
4 Ibid.
5 Willard, 26.

Why does God want the kingdom of God to come to the world through you? For your benefit. We maximize what we can be by cooperating with God through His rule in our lives. When we submit to the rule of God, or the kingdom of God, our lives change, and people can see God at work.

I was explaining this to my wife the other day. The marriage that she and I have today (one of the most sacred and delightful things in my life) is the result of my submission to God's rule over thirty years ago about how to be married. Back then, I was making a mess of all my dating relationships, wanting a number of them to move towards marriage but they kept exploding. But then God showed me through a godly mentor what it would look like if I was willing to be married God's way—what I would have to do, what I would have to change, what I would have to act like, what I could no longer do towards the person I was "in love with." This was all a revelation and a completely different way of living. Submitting to God's rule in my life in the area of romance, dating, and marriage was a very strange thing. But entering God's kingdom in the area of romance, dating, and marriage has been one of the most amazing things I have ever done. I met my wife a few years after I agreed to learn God's way of treating a woman in a maturing love relationship.

The fact that I decided to submit to God's governance over how I treated a woman has made all the difference in our marriage. She has only known me as the person who submits to God's way of treating a woman—someone who is seeking the kingdom of God in this area. She does not know the sarcastic, demanding, self-focused, egotistical man I was before submitting to the rule of God in this area of my life. I told her that we would not be having the joy, love, delight, and fun in our marriage if I had stayed the same and "done" marriage my way. We would be like so many couples we meet who are critical, sarcastic, discouraged, and defeated in their marriage. Ask God to bring His kingdom into every part of your life. It will seem strange and different, but it is the best thing that could happen to you. It really will transform your life.

Jesus wants us to have a kingdom discussion with God and live out what it means to be citizens of heaven on this earth every day. God's kingdom shows up when His followers let Him flow through them by loving, serving, and using the power of God, bringing justice beyond what is culturally accepted. This is how we will show the people of this world the reality of the next world. Entering into the kingdom of God means we submit to God's way of living in the various areas of our life. We no longer do what we think is best; we actively learn, practice, and act God's way in our finances, in our work, in our family, and with our personal habits. When we enter into His kingdom, God changes us and empowers us to live a life that is beyond us. Too many people are trying to accept the forgiveness of God through Christ and then still doing life the way they think is best. That is not seeking first the kingdom of God and His righteousness. The blessings don't lie down that path.

In the time of the apostle Paul, the city of Philippi was a Roman colony, meaning that it was an extension of Rome outside of the actual city of Rome. Roman law, Roman culture, and Roman rules applied in every colony and city within its boundaries. Paul wrote to the Christians in Philippi explaining that they were actually an extension of heaven, just as their city was an extension of Rome, though a long way from Rome. As Christians, we are to live by heavenly power, heavenly culture, and heavenly rules, and when we do, the kingdom of God becomes visible on this earth. Paul said it this way, "For our citizenship is in heaven, from which also we eagerly wait for a Savior, the Lord Jesus Christ." (Phil 3:20)

The implications of this verse in Philippians are immense. Paul is telling us that we, as believers in Jesus Christ, are a part of a different structure and country. We are a part of a kingdom—God's kingdom. This kingdom, which is coming, already exists in the lives and deeds of its citizens. Notice in Matthew 3:2, John the Baptist began proclaiming, "Repent, for the kingdom of heaven is at hand." The people were to make themselves ready to join a different culture. Instead of one that was dog-eat-dog and selfish to the core, this new kingdom would be built on God's ideals, one based on "loving God with all your heart, soul, mind, and strength, and loving your neighbor as yourself." Wherever Jesus was on the earth, the kingdom was made manifest. This prayer means, then, that wherever the Christian believer is, they will be a kingdom agent for God. Not just talking about God, but living, loving, and deciding based upon God's ideals. Until God actually splits the skies and blasts the trumpet marking the physical return of Christ, we are God's kingdom agents spreading the kingdom of God through our deeds, conversations, and invitations. As we wait for the king to come and set up the physical manifestation of the kingdom of God, He wants to talk with us daily, even hourly, about how to let God flow through us to display the kingdom of God in the world.

When I talk to God about His kingdom coming, that is His will being done on earth as it is in heaven, I talk about letting Him flow through my actions, words, my attitudes.

I talk about the areas where I am doing life my way and what He wants me to do instead. I talk about submitting to God's rule or governance in my life in the various areas of my life. *"Lord, is there a particular part of my life that You want me to make sure I am doing things Your way?"* Is your work life, your finances, your family life a reflection of living in God's kingdom, or do they reflect the way you learned how to handle that part of life? When I have these discussions with God asking that His rule and governance would come to an area of my life, it begins with three basic elements of kingdom behavior, and then may move out to the specifics of that particular arena of life. What are the three basic areas of kingdom living?

- Kingdom actions

- Kingdom character

- Kingdom boundaries

Realize that each of these kingdom expressions must be sourced in God or else it loses the distinctive element of God's kingdom. He is the one who will give the actions that are kingdom actions—He defines them. He is the one who will develop kingdom character in and through you. And He is the one who will warn, enforce, and provide the power to turn away from God's negative boundaries. We run across these kingdom elements under different areas in Scripture. Let's examine them in more detail.

Kingdom actions. God tells us in various places in Scripture that He wants to produce fruit in and through our lives as evidence to others that God is real and at work in our life. (John 5:1–8; Gal 5:22–23) He wants to prompt us to love, joy, peace, patience, kindness, goodness, gentleness, faithfulness, and self-control. Letting God add huge amounts of these qualities into our various relationships changes the nature of our life. It makes sense that God wants to discuss with us regularly about what we will let Him do through us since He knows these qualities produce good "fruit" in our lives and in the lives of others. I have given a prayer exercise that allows you and God to talk about how, who, what, and when to do these in your life at the end of this chapter.

Kingdom character. In the opening verses of the Sermon on the Mount, God tells us what the character qualities of the kingdom are, essentially Jesus' character, as found in the Beatitudes. (Matt 5:1-11) They are: poor in spirit (humble); mourning (processing pain); meekness (power under control); hunger and thirst after righteousness (desire for good); merciful (not demanding vengeance); pure in heart (positive, pure, and edifying thought life); peacemakers (bringing harmony, order, and calm); persecution for righteousness and Christ (establishing healthy boundaries). It is these qualities pouring through our lives that mark us as citizens of heaven. Jesus tells us that these qualities are the key to being blessed in His kingdom. We desperately need to cooperate with God in developing and pouring these qualities through our lives. It is the growth of these qualities that allows our individual lives to be blessed. These qualities also allow cities, regions, and nations to be blessed and live in harmony and peace. Use the prayer exercises at the end of this chapter to dialogue with God about developing as His kingdom agent in these ways.

Kingdom boundaries. God tells us way back in Exodus that there are certain behaviors that will threaten our community, destroy individuals, and damage ourselves.

We understand these as the Ten Commandments. (Ex 20:1-17) The Ten Commandments are a win-lose, red line—the markers that tell us when we are no longer playing fair with others. Our society needs Christians to live ethical lives that do not violate these moral boundaries. This type of living will become evidence of kingdom living. I have also included prayer exercises for this aspect of "Your kingdom come" at the end of the chapter.

Today, we are stuck in the deeply depressing and sinful here and now, and we need evidence that there is something better, something beyond this life. Our lives as kingdom agents give hope to others and testifies to the wonder of God's kingdom. God tells His followers to interact with Him in their prayer life about how they can become a channel for the kingdom that is present right here, through them. If we are to become kingdom agents, we have to talk with God about what He wants us to do to be effective. Now let me say that becoming a kingdom agent is very practical and personal. Sometimes it involves loving your spouse when you don't want to. Sometimes you may need to volunteer at a soup kitchen, even though your time is tight. Sometimes He may ask you to go and talk with a neighbor. Sometimes He wants you to be a great employee at work, working as to the Lord, not men. (Col 3:23–24)

True intimacy with God takes more than just good intentions; it takes real action. In the Lord's Prayer, Jesus suggests we do something with God that is really different than we are naturally prone to do. He says that we should have a discussion regularly (daily or hourly) with God about what kingdom actions, qualities, rules, and speech should appear in our world through us. God has specific ideas in mind and He wants to talk with you about all these things.

Without prayer, we can miss out on God's assignments and the subsequent blessings, even miracles, that come out of obedience.

We can ask, *"God, what type of kingdom action do you want to do through my life so that others will know you are God?"* Let God direct the answer instead of you trying to decide what God may want to do. I am always amazed at how God directs me. I have watched God supply money, heal people, convict people, embrace them with love, encourage them, and touch them. His demonstrations of His kingdom are different than I would have thought in many cases.

Remember, this was Jesus' response when He was asked by His disciples about how to have the intimate, personal connection and relationship with God that He had. The disciples saw in Jesus' prayer life a different way of relating to God, and they wanted that. Jesus did not discourage this line of inquiry; instead, He encouraged them by talking about the types of conversations and prayer exercises that disciples need to have with God if they are going to be truly intimate with Him. Praying to make a kingdom difference here and now is one of them.

Prayer for God's Future Kingdom

Now let's spend some time talking about how to dialogue with God about the return of Christ and the coming kingdom of God in a future sense. This topic has captivated, energized, and fascinated Christians down through the centuries of the church. God wants us to be ready at all times for His return. (Matt 25:13) What is also clear from this section is that God wants us to be kingdom agents while we await His return. And being kingdom agents means expressing faith, love, and the hope of salvation. (1 Thess 5:1-5)

Our active participation in prayer and loving, righteous actions are the ways that we participate in moving the kingdom of God closer to breaking into our world. In every generation, the Lord's return to the earth is possible. Jesus said that He would return (Acts 1:8, 11), and when He does, He will initiate His kingdom, which is spoken of throughout the Scriptures. (Rev 19:11-16; 20:4). All Christians down through ages hope for Jesus Christ's return and the setting up of His kingdom on the earth. We may argue about the order of events or the connection of one event to others, but we all believe that Jesus is coming back to set up His kingdom. His kingdom will be one where He will reign and the moral elements that He has established will be set up. The markers of the return of Christ and the setting up of His kingdom consist of ten different events specified in Scripture. The Bible clearly says that these ten events will take place and will mark the end of history as we know it. These events will happen in and around the return of Christ.

To pray "Your kingdom come" in a future sense is to have a discussion with God about these ten events. We know that our efforts as Christians to be kingdom agents will not finish the task of bringing in the kingdom of God, only Jesus Himself can do that; so, we long for the time when Jesus splits the sky and brings the fullness of His kingdom to this earth. Every Christian has a longing in their heart for the return of Christ. And in every age and every period, Christians have believed that they have seen these elements gathering in their lifetime. For example, if you were a Christian from AD 50-70, there was the destruction of Jerusalem and the rise of Nero. If you were in the city of Rome in AD 410, you would point to Alaric and the invasion of Rome. If you were in England in 1803, you would point to Napoleon. And many pointed to Hitler in 1935–1944 as the Antichrist. God has not told us when these events will occur but that they will occur eventually. I believe that the Devil also does not know the time, the place, or the person, and so sets about readying his plans in every generation to bring the world to an end.

When we dialogue with God, we should discuss areas of sin and darkness being observed in our day and age. Are they happening in your nation or part of the world? What are you as a Christian supposed to do to remain faithful and prepare for the return of Christ in your vocation and situation? How are you to respond to the events taking place in your nation and your region that connect to the scriptural events? We are more than just spectators in this grand program of God. We need to know how we are to prepare against the Devil's work—what we can do to occupy the time until He comes. The kingdom coming is the fullest expression of God's will be done on earth as it is in heaven, so we wait for that day. We pray for that day. We work to bring about that day if at all possible. (Matt 24:12; 1 Thess 5:1–5)

Prayer Exercises

There are four prayer lists you can pray through to see what God wants to do in and through you as His kingdom agent. Decide if God wants you to pray through the Fruit of the Spirit, the Beatitudes, or the Ten Commandments to enrich your relationships and life here on earth today. The last prayer exercise is designed for you to work with the Ten Events that will usher in His future coming. Enjoy these!

Fruit of the Spirit

First, focus on one of the various relationships of your life: Work, Marriage, Family, Church, Personal Development, Finances, God, Friends, Enemies. Allow God to guide you as to which one needs your attention today. Pray slowly through the fruits of the Spirit. Ask, *"Lord, which of the fruit do you want me to let you do through me in this relationship?"*

- Is it Love?
- Is it Joy?
- Is it Peace?
- Is it Patience?
- Is it Kindness?
- Is it Gentleness?
- Is it Goodness?
- Is it Faithfulness?
- Is it Self-Control?

He will highlight one of these qualities to you. Then ask, *"What does that look like, Lord?"* God will begin to put into your mind ways that you could be more loving in one of the arenas of your life. Plan on discussing these ideas that appear in your head and when to do them.

Letting God show the kingdom through your life will mean that you may act differently than you have in the past. This is about having the kingdom of God show up in your world through you. He wants your life to be a laboratory of new marvels, where He gets glory from how you let Him work through your life. Pray and ask God what you could do that would allow more love, joy, peace, patience, kindness, goodness, gentleness, faithfulness, and self-control to flow into the various relationships of your life.

I will often take a piece of paper or my phone and ask God to show me twenty ways I can show love or joy or peace to whomever He wants me to display it. As I dialogue with God about these twenty ways, I am forced to stretch beyond my comfort zone with this person. That is where it gets interesting. When I did this exercise recently, God and I had quite the discussion about how He wanted to inject more love and joy into my family. One of the ideas that popped into my mind was to start making videos and photos of my daily life and posting them to a family text group we have. They have been such a hit and everybody has this closeness because we all react and talk about the stuff we all put up there. One of my girls said it was like sitting around the kitchen table and having a conversation. It has significantly increased the love and joy in our family. By-the-way, my new book *The Keys for Grapeness: Growing a Spirit-led Life* talks all about this, and my hope is that it will give you more clarity on what love, joy, peace, and so on, actually looks like in a practical, day-to-day sense.

Just the other day, I was prompted to love my wife and family more in the area of finances by being self-controlled at a new level. When I started writing the answers to this question, I was surprised by what God began to suggest. The things I could tangibly do were to: save on the phone bill; reduce going out to eat; look at other job options; learn new skills to enhance my position; watch the budget more carefully; make a tighter budget; and explore other business options. My mind became a whirl of ideas and possibilities, and God has begun to bring some of these about so that I can partner with Him to bring more love, joy, peace, patience, kindness, goodness, and so on, into our financial life.

Beatitudes

We know from the Bible the Lord wants us to grow in the character of Christ. It is the key to having a blessed life. Ask the Lord about which of these qualities He is currently focused on developing in you. Pause and then slowly and prayerfully read through the Beatitudes listening for the Lord's prompting about one of the qualities. *"Lord, which of these do you want to develop in me?"*

- Poor in spirit (humble, grateful, teachable, self-assured)

- Mournful (grieving pain, losses, wounds, and guilt)

- Meek (power under control, impulse control, thoughtful requests, and wise adaptations)

- Hungry and thirsty for righteousness (desperate desire to bring about what is right)

- Merciful (not demanding every ounce of vengeance)

- Pure in heart (positive, pure, and edifying thought life)

- Peacemaker (reconciliatory, bringing harmony, order, and calm everywhere I go)

- Persecution for righteousness and for Christ

When God has highlighted one of the qualities, ask Him what are twenty ways you can show more of that quality in and through your life. Be prepared for insight that you and God might come up with to lead a different kind of life. We do not realize how the lack of these qualities holds us back from the life we want and could have.

I was talking with a young man recently, who knew that God was trying to get his attention about his ego and arrogance. He had a hard time believing that his ideas and desires were not better than any boss, friend, partner, or colleague. This is why God has given him a boss who doesn't seem to care about his ideas. He knows that he hears God telling him to serve his boss without rancor and dismissiveness, but he has such a hard time not being listened to and followed. This will be a battle until this young man embraces the need for humility over the better idea.

I was working with a middle-aged man, who had given into excess and impurity, rather than face the pain of rebuilding his life. God is providing this man with a trial that will be the best thing that ever happened to him if he continues with the program. God wants this man to be a shining example of purity of mind and passionate pursuit of righteousness. I am encouraged by his desire to make progress and do what is needed to develop these qualities of a great life.

Ten Commandments

If we are going to express the kingdom of God here on earth, we must live within the basic boundaries of the Ten Commandments. I recommend that we recite and pray through the Ten Commandments each day and allow God to point out any areas where our lives are outside these boundaries. Let me use the shortened version that I taught my children when they were small. You can look at the longer versions in Exodus 20:3-17 and Deuteronomy 5:6-21. I usually recite the two great commandments before these ten to remember that the goal is to love God, others, and ourselves righteously, and the Ten Commandments are what Love for God, Others, and Self cannot mean. (Matt 22:36-39)

- You shall love the Lord Your God with all your heart, soul, mind, and strength, and your neighbor as yourself

- You shall have no other gods before Me

- You shall not make for yourselves any graven images

- You shall not take the name of the Lord your God in vain

- Remember the Sabbath Day, to keep it holy

- Honor your Father and your Mother

- You shall not murder

- You shall not commit adultery

- You shall not steal

- You shall not bear false witness against your neighbor

- You shall not covet anything that belongs to your neighbor

I have had many fruitful discussions with God over the Great Commandments and the Ten Commandments as I evaluated what He wanted me to do in particular situations and with particular people. These commands are edges to the path of life, and we should pay attention to them and discuss their implications with God regularly.

The Ten Events

These are the ten events that mark the kingdom of God's future coming. They form a prayer guide in regard to the return of Christ and an opportunity to look at Scripture and discuss with God how to be ready if it happens in your lifetime. Remember, different Christians put these ten events in different arrangements, but these will take place eventually as God moves His kingdom forward to the place where it will burst into our world. Look up these verses and read them carefully, making notes about what God is telling you to look for and how you are to respond. What are the things you must to do prepare? Use these truths as a prayer guide to interact with God about these issues. Look up the Scriptures and be keen to discuss with God when these elements begin to move forward in your generation.

- Wars and Rumors of Wars: Matthew 24:6
- The Great Falling Away: 2 Thessalonians 2:3
- The Great Tribulation: Matthew 24:21-22
- The Antichrist: 2 Thessalonians 2:3-10; Daniel 9:25-27
- The Abomination of Desolations: Matthew 24:15-21, 2 Thessalonians 2:1-12
- The Rapture of Believers: 1 Thessalonians 4:13-18; 2 Thessalonians 2:1-4: Matthew 24:36-41; Daniel 12:1
- The Return of Christ: Revelation 19:11-19: Matthew 24:29-31; 2 Thessalonians 1:5-10
- Resurrection of the Dead: Revelation 20:4-6: Daniel 12:2, 13
- The Millennium: Revelation 20:2-5; Isaiah 11:2-10
- Judgment Day: Revelation 20:11-15
- The New Heavens and the New Earth: Revelation 21:1-22:5

Some other questions you can include in your daily discussion with God are:

- *How can I bring the kingdom into the world through my life right now?*
- *How can I do God's will on this earth today? What does He want me to do?*
- *How can I love God with all my heart, soul, mind, and strength?*
- *How can I love my neighbor as myself?*

The next chapter covers the topic of provision, which introduces a huge arena for dialogue with God, not to mention that it sets a wonderful stage for Him to work miracles in your life and in others' lives through you. This dialogue that Jesus wants us to have is proof that God really cares about the smallest of details in our lives. And He wants to give you everything you need to succeed as His kingdom agent. Let's find out more about this.

5.

GOD, WILL YOU PROVIDE FOR ME FOR YOUR GLORY?

"Give us this day our daily bread." (Matt 6:11)

I AM MORE CONVINCED THAN EVER THAT GOD WANTS TO DO AMAZING, MIRACULOUS THINGS for us and through us on this earth to prove to a skeptical world that He is alive and ready to work with those who will respond to His call. In the last chapter, we learned that Jesus wants us to dialogue with God about us as His kingdom agents today and our role to prepare for the approach of His return. Doing kingdom exercises allows us to be ready for His return and prepares us to be in the game, rather than on the sidelines watching.

Matthew 6:11 tells us to ask God for all the things our lives need. This is not just about bread and water, clothing and housing, and so forth, although Jesus does want us to dialogue with God about those things. It actually ties into the previous verse, *"Your will be done on earth as it is in heaven."* Based on what we learned in the last chapter, we can surmise that Jesus is telling us to have a detailed dialogue with God about what we need in order to accomplish our life purpose and mission on this earth—that is, to ask about what we specifically need to accomplish what He wants us to do here. Yes, Jesus knows what we need, but He wants us to ask for it so lest we forget where the provision comes from. We are to engage with Him about the whole of our life.

This prayer between you and God is not for you to just say a one-sentence line and expect God to fill in the blanks. I heard the story of a woman who got tired of praying over the same list every night, so she nailed her prayer list to the wall above her bed and pointed to it when she got into bed and prayed, "God, I need that stuff. Amen." That kind of short-cut praying is what many people do with the Lord's Prayer. They think that if they just say, "Give me this day my daily bread," then all of their needs will be covered. No, this sentence covers the topic of provision for our life mission here on earth, which introduces a huge arena for dialogue with God. (Not to mention that it sets a huge stage for God to work in your life and in others' lives as He works through you.)

Years ago, I was challenged to pray about my life and my needs in a completely different way. It was not connected to this sentence in Matthew 6, but I later realized that this is what this prayer exercise is all about. I was challenged to write down exactly what I want and need if life were to be perfect (i.e., relationally fruitful) five years in the future.

I looked at the ten relationships of my life and began detailing what I would want my marriage to be like, my work to be like, my children to be like, as well as my finances and contribution to society. I took three months to work and pray through each relational category, and began to ask God for answers and solutions to each of those ideas every day. If, as I prayed, I sensed my goal or idea was not right, I changed it to the right one. I remember telling God what I really needed in order to make my family work, my job work, and to meet my girls' impending college expenses. It was amazing to have this back-and-forth dialogue with God over months and now years. What is truly amazing, and you might even say miraculous, is that God provided all that I needed. He truly did the impossible in answer to my prayers about my needs. I asked Him for what I needed to build a righteous, god-honoring life, and He did it. I am still blown away at the fact that God provided ninety percent of what was on the paper. And the stuff He did not provide, He did something better, or else I realized that I didn't need those things like I thought I did. I was offered jobs I was not seeking. I was invited into conversations with my girls that were deep, life changing, and incredibly critical. I was directed to let go of rules and issues to let a relationship grow. And I was encouraged to try new activities that I had not considered for decades.

I want you to realize that just saying "Give us this day our daily bread" is not enough. It goes beyond the material. I understand from the Scriptures that God thinks relationally, not materially. He tells us that the Great Commandments are to love God with all our heart, soul, mind, and strength, and our neighbor as ourselves, which are relational commands. (Matt 22:37–39) God wants us to fill our world with amazing and wonderful relationships. He knows that you need all kinds of things, qualities, actions, and attitudes in order to live for Him. Every single day you have emotional needs, mental needs, financial needs, relational needs, and physical needs that you must have God supply in order to accomplish what He wants you to do here on earth. He will supply what you need if you will ask for it, and then use what He supplies for His glory.

The Concept of "God Kits"

I have found many people only want God to provide finished blessings, rather than to use the raw materials God provides. I like to call these "God kits." Instead of providing perfect children, piles of money, the best job ever, or a problem-free life, God has provided jobs, ideas, opportunities, problems, and people that have been the keys to getting my needs met. When I dialogue with God about my needs, He is willing to give me the answers in unique ways.

For example, when I prayed for the money to send my girls to college, God gave me a second job that allowed us to get them through without debt. I prayed for a depth of relationship with God, so that I would be loved and guided by Him every day. He has opened up the Word of God in ways that are so personal and so clear it has changed my decision-making process, changed my ideas, and ultimately changed my life as He has pulled me close.

I prayed that God would take mine and Dana's marriage to the next level of intimacy and joy, and He has provided a sweetness between my wife and I that is one of the most awesome things in my world. Just a note on the marriage front, one of the ideas that God gave me that changed and deepened my marriage was when He directed me to say or text every positive thing I thought about Dana whenever it came to me. Whenever I think, "Isn't it great that she did the laundry?" I text her that I really appreciate that she did that. Whenever I think, "I am so glad I am not dating and trying to find a mate," I tell her that I am so glad to be married to her and not out in the dating world. Our marriage is full of positive affirmations of all the things that she does right (and it is a lot). There is no room for negative issues. The exciting thing is that she has started doing the same thing. Do you know what it is like to be in a relationship where every time you are with that person you are reminded of the things you are doing right? This is heaven on earth.

All of this takes writing, praying, talking, thinking, and dialoguing with God, and sometimes others, too, to formulate what you think you need in order to live the life God has planned for you. There is often so much potential God has for us that we never really explore. Reach out and dream with God. Ask Him, "What do you want me to go after, Lord, and what will I need to do that?"

Prayer Exercise

What Is Your Ideal Life?

I just spent the most delightful time talking with God about the next three years and what the goals, ideas, plans, accomplishments, and progress He and I can make in that time. Life is not meant to be static but dynamic. Ask God to thrust you forward toward righteous goals and watch Him answer. I do this exercise constantly but especially in December and January, as this changing of the year focuses my mind on what God would have me go after in the next three to five years. If we are not careful, we will not ask God for all that He would give us if our goals were larger. (Matt 7:7) I have also found that I need to think out three to five years into the future to turn off the "how" issue. We are often so worried about the how that we do not spend enough time with God on the what! What is the dream that He has put in your heart? What could you accomplish with Him if you let go of the fear? Ask God for what you need.

If life were ideal in the key relational arenas, what would be happening? If we ask for it in the present, we immediately think it is impossible, so we stop dreaming. But I know that much of what is not possible this week, this month, or this year is possible in three to five years, and we need to ask God for it.

Another way to say it is this: If God were going to use your life as an example of a miracle, what would your life look like in three to five years? You are just talking about what you need if your life is to be maximized in a righteous way. Use the grid below as a prompt to get you to think about what your ideal life would look like for you in three to five years. Spend some time making a list like I did with these ten relationships in life. Spend an hour, a day, a month, or three months and really imagine what would make things great in those areas! When you start this exercise, you will probably jot some selfish things down, but as you go over and over each relationship, you will begin to describe positive, righteous, and godly ideals. Keep praying, keep talking, keep working this out with God as your guide.

As you pray through them, expect God to work them out. That's where faith comes in. Write down twenty specific things you would need for each category. This will really stretch you into thinking, praying, and dreaming big with God. Get ready to experience the miracles He will provide to help you get there. His creativity really is unbelievable. Try it!

The Ten Basic Relationships of Life

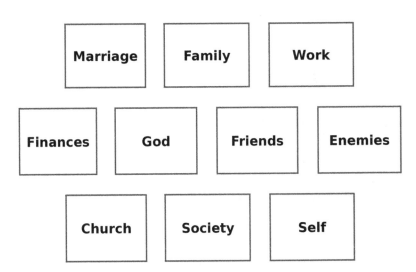

Next, we will talk about something very important that will require a lot of dialoguing and working back and forth with God in order to progress in intimacy with Him. What is Jesus really saying when He talks about forgiveness for ourselves and others? What do we do about all the hurts others have inflicted upon us, as well as those we have brought upon ourselves? Let's explore this in the next chapter and see what God wants to say regarding the topic of forgiveness.

6.

GOD, HELP ME TO FORGIVE MYSELF AND OTHERS!

"And forgive us our debts, as we also have forgiven our debtors." (Matt 6:12)

GOD WANTS TO DO MORE IN US AND THROUGH US THAN WE CAN POSSIBLY IMAGINE. HE wants our relationships to thrive and prosper and to bless us. The last chapter taught us that God wants us to ask Him for provision, but not just the daily kind. Rather, He invites us to ask for whatever is necessary to fulfill the mission He has for us on earth and use it for His glory so that He can use us and bless us.

This next verse, Matthew 6:12, is as equally rich and deep, and I could literally write a whole other book just about this topic! In fact, I just might! What is Jesus really saying when He talks about forgiving our debts as we have also forgiven our debtors? He invites us to have lots of conversations with God about what we have done against ourselves, what others do against us, and what we do against others in order to move toward true intimacy with God and others.

It is true that we will do wrong and feel wronged in this world. This is not the ideal world that was given to Adam and Eve. It has suffered from the ravages of rebellion and sin. In this part of the Lord's Prayer, Jesus instructs us to have an extensive dialogue with God about confession and forgiveness, knowing that He has left us in a sinful world, and knowing that true intimacy cannot occur where there is no forgiveness. The surface idea of this verse seems to be about us gaining forgiveness, but the second part indicates the need for our active participation in forgiving others. We can only imagine that Jesus, as a man, had interesting discussions with God about the selfishness, sin, and difficulties He saw all around Him in the towns and villages He visited. I'm sure it grieved Him very much.

We know when we are withholding forgiveness or mercy from another person, don't we? Or how about when we are self-condemning and holding ourselves hostage to shame and guilt? Our spirit within us tells us this. We know it because there is an unsettled feeling deep inside us as our soul wars against the Holy Spirit. This conflict within us— the ill thoughts that swirl around in our minds about the other person, or intense waves of regret and shame about the things we've done, are all symptoms that forgiveness is needed. God wants to free us from this, but it will take some focus, time, and vulnerability in prayer.

Many people are unwilling to have these discussions with God. They would rather just stay angry with Him or the other person and remain imprisoned in their own emotional cage. It's not supposed to be that way. As this sentence tells us, we will need to receive the forgiveness of

God and give God's love and forgiveness to others. Why? Because without these two graces, we will not be able to plumb the depths of intimacy with God, and we will not be able to enter into other relationships at great depth, which is His desire for us. We have to be willing to be forgiven and willing to forgive.

The Healing Process of Forgiveness

Allow God to walk you through healing that comes through forgiveness. It is not sufficient to just say "forgive us our debts, as we have also forgiven our debtors." When we are talking with God about forgiveness, we are talking with Him about the sins of others, our own sins, why He is permitting sin, and how to access His grace and mercy to operate in this fallen world.

I have found that dealing adequately with the issue of forgiveness involves at least six different topics and prayer exercises. First, the issue of confession of our own sins. Second, the forgiveness and release of bitterness because of what others have done to us. Third, forgiving ourselves for what we did or did not do which brought about our present state. Fourth, setting goals for the rest of our lives so we don't stay stuck in the present or the past. Fifth, letting God love us in new ways and allowing His love to flow through us in more powerful and very specific ways. Sixth, bringing a new peace to our life by embracing harmony, order, and calm. These issues of confession, forgiveness of others and ourselves, setting goals, practicing love, and championing peace are all part of the discussion we will regularly need to have with God, which will change our lives and give us the type of intimate life with Him that Jesus enjoyed here.

Let me go into these areas in more detail so that you can open up your prayer life to these discussions and exercises.

1. Confession discussions with God:

The first aspect of forgiveness deals with the forgiveness of our own sins, and we do that through confession. Having a discussion with God about forgiveness usually starts with a willingness to let God show us how we may have been at fault in some, or all, of our present troubles. (Gal 6:7) This part of the discussion will involve letting God convict us of sins that we have committed. One way to do this is to pray through a biblical list of sins, like the Seven Deadly Sins, pausing after each one to see if God brings up that sin as something you need to talk with Him about. The Seven Deadly Sins are pride, envy, anger, lust, sloth, gluttony, and greed.

As you pray, ask, *"Lord, have I committed any pride?"* Then pause and see if God brings anything to mind. If He does bring something to mind, then have a discussion with Him about what it was that He brought to your mind, agreeing with Him (confess) about the issue. Thank Him for paying for that sin and selfishness through the life and death of Jesus Christ. Continue working through the other sins, really pausing after each one so you allow God to bring something to mind.

It's important, also, to spend time realizing that this is exactly why Jesus Christ came to the earth. He came to live the perfect life here so that He could give up what He had earned willingly. This is how we are able to enjoy relationship with God and a future in heaven. Because of what Jesus did, we are forgiven. (Rom 8:1) We are not under the penalty of sin any longer; we are loved by God and now look to please Him. We are not forgiven because of something we do, but because of what He did.

Some have found it helpful to do a slightly different spiritual exercise to heighten their awareness of God in confession. They use the relationships of their life as the guide to pray through. There is a much fuller discussion of this process in my book *Spiritual Disciplines of a C.H.R.I.S.T.I.A.N.* under the chapter called "Confession."

2. **Forgiveness and release of bitterness—letting go of what others have done to us.**

When Jesus says "forgive us our debts, as we also have forgiven our debtors," He is inviting us to dialogue with God about our wounds, guilt, and pain. Are there people in your life that you have not released for the things they've done to you? If so, they still are a bitter pill in your soul. This dialogue with God will involve letting Him search the arenas of your life to see if there are people that you have not forgiven for their sins and slights. Talk with God about the relational arenas of your life (God, Marriage, Family, Self, Work, Friends, Church, Society, Finances) and let Him deal with the people who have become enemies and attackers. This may require many discussions and interactions with God.

Let me give you a few exercises that I recommend in this area of releasing bitterness and vengeance. As you pray through the various aspects of your life, if God brings a particular person or organization to mind as someone who has deeply hurt you and you have not released them to God for the appropriate justice, then follow these steps in prayer:

Exercise #1—Assess the nature of the offense against you. (Matt 23:34; Acts 16:35-40; Matt 18:15-18; Col 3:13; Acts 6:1-3) Was it a personal offense, a relational offense, an organizational offense, a civil offense, or a criminal offense? It can be very helpful to take the time to classify the offense, because we can inflate an offense against us as a criminal offense, but it really was just someone being rude. The response to a criminal offense (something which damages or destroys others) is significantly different than a relational offense (something that damages our relationship). This is where we might have a discussion with God about the nature of the offense and how to move past it, and what or who you might alert if it is serious enough so as to protect others.

Exercise #2—Hire God as your hit man. (Rom 12:17-19) God tells us that we were not meant to carry the responsibility for vengeance against those who have deeply hurt or wounded us. We need to hand the job of vengeance and punishment to God and His representatives. I have helped many people have dialogues with God about the people who have wounded them, handing them over to God's all-knowing and all-powerful abilities. If we continue to try and carry out our schemes, then God will not handle it. But if we get out of the way and get on with our lives, then He will take whatever actions are necessary. We can trust Him, and we need to move on from allowing these issues to define us.

Exercise #3—Educate your offender. (Luke 17:3) We may need to have a discussion with God about talking with our offender as a part of our healing. God says that if someone sins against us, then we are to rebuke them (educate them). There is often an appropriate time in our healing when we can and should let the people who hurt us know what they did to us. Do not educate your offender if doing so would put you in greater danger of being hurt. But there is often a place in your discussions with God where He wants you to let the people who hurt you know that they did not win in what they were trying to do. He did this in Joseph's life in Genesis 50:20. He had Joseph wait until after his father, Jacob, was dead and then he told his brothers that he, Joseph, knew they had sold him into slavery. It was evil, but God redeemed it for good so that all of their families could be saved. This education process of Joseph's brothers was years in the making and surely required many discussions with God to bring about.

Exercise #4—Look for good to come from it. (Rom 8:28) God is powerful enough and wise enough to turn any evil that may happen to us into something good in our life. This is not something that we can usually see right away, especially when the evil and destruction is still new and devastating. This idea that God can bring good out of tragedy takes lots of talks with God and lots of looking for how God might redeem an incident. Ask God to show you the opportunities, pathways, insights, ideas, and relationships that could lead to this wound being a good thing. Remember that God's good things often do not appear in our lives as completed projects. They come as small problems, little ideas, or new opportunities that need work, learning, effort, and resources to develop—God kits. Pray, *"Oh God, show me what these good things are, and how I can embrace them to move past this pain."*

3. **Forgiving ourselves for what we did or didn't do, which brought about our present state.**

Going deep with God and working through forgiveness will involve mourning the wounds of the past that altered your future. If we are going to ask God to forgive our transgressions, then it logically means we must also forgive ourselves. Jesus tells us that we need to process the pain of the realities of our world in order to move forward by mourning what could have been, what we've lost, and what went wrong—*"Blessed are those who mourn, for they will be comforted."* (Matt 5:4)

Many times, people hold themselves to an unrealistic standard. Romans 8:1 says that God is not condemning them, because of what He had Christ do for them on the cross. People need to forgive themselves for what they did or didn't do, what they didn't know, or what they did or didn't say. You are not perfect, and if you are going to be able to get past the mistakes of the past or present, you must forgive yourself, even as God has forgiven you in Christ. This element will take many discussions and verses to help you see that God is for you and not against you.

I have two really good prayer exercises that will help you walk through this process of forgiving yourself. Work on these exercises until you feel good and grounded in this area of forgiveness. It's important that you get to this place of forgiving yourself.

Exercise #1—Understand how God sees you. To start the process of truly forgiving yourself, you must get to a place where you see yourself as God sees you. The truth about how He sees us is much more important than what we think to be true, isn't it? There are numerous biblical truths about your standing in Christ as a Christian. There is immense truth and power about your standing within the family of God. He loves you and you must embrace this fact in order to accomplish the mission of righteousness and love that God has for you in this world. It is also the only way to enjoy Him and others fully. I've listed the first two here, but there are so many others I want you to look at. See the Appendix "Understanding How God Sees You."

- I am God's child (John 1:12). Having believed in Jesus as God, He accepts me as His child.

- I am Christ's friend (John 15:15). He calls me His friend and He is willing to reveal His plans to me.

We have much to be thankful for as children of God. The rights and privileges we get for aligning ourselves with Christ are immense! Next time you get down on yourself or feel unworthy or disqualified in some way because of things you've done in your past, go back to these verses and remind yourself who you are and whose you are. He forgives you so that you can forgive yourself. This is one of the most powerful things you can do.

Exercise #2—Get it all out. Many of us need to have discussions with God about unfair treatment, broken relationships, lost opportunities, abuse, and the injustices we've experienced. These issues are not handled in one discussion within a few minutes—they require longer discussions with God, and sometimes these may be heated, as we don't always see why this had to happen. Rest assured, God can handle our heat and is not put off by it. I always deeply enjoy the discussion between Jeremiah and God in Jeremiah 15, where the prophet poetically calls God a liar and deceptive and wants to know what God is going to do about the promises He made! (Jer 15:15-21)

I have often encouraged people to go out to a park, the ocean, or any solitary place, and cry out to God about the pain and hurt. When there is pain in your soul, it needs to come out. Sometimes it is expressed in crying, sometimes in yelling and shouting, sometimes in running, strenuous work, or even cleaning. The Jewish time table for mourning was at least forty days following the loss of a loved one. The person was not expected to be normal or even in communication with his friends for that length of time so as to deal with the loss. Our culture wants to be done with pain, loss, and wounds in four minutes! It is just not healthy or possible. Take the time to wallow in the difficulties of the loss and pain.

Abraham Lincoln had a favorite method for dealing with pain and loss that we can learn from. Take a piece of paper and write a letter to the person expressing everything you really feel and want to say with all the strength, emotion, and venom you feel. You won't send this letter, but you need to get your emotions out of you. I usually suggest that the letter be destroyed in a few hours or days after it has been written. We have records of many letters in Lincoln's desk that were never sent; they didn't need to be once he got the pain and disappointment out of his soul.

In the midst of tragedy, our emotions are like a tornado which swirls around in our soul, changing from one emotion to the next within a few moments. We are not able to really understand all that we feel except that our emotions are strong and always in flux. This is all a part of your prayer time in which you talk to God about all that you are feeling and experiencing. God is not expecting you to have the answers or even be open to His answers; He just wants to be a part of your process. If you do not get these hurts out of your soul, they will begin to warp the person you are really supposed to become. Stuffed emotions and pain will twist us and they will find their way to the outside world in some way. It is better to bring it out in writing, discussions, prayer, singing, or sharing with trusted friends than to become a twisted version of our selves.

4. **Setting goals for the rest of our lives—don't stay stuck in the present or the past.**

Working through forgiveness and being healthy after we have suffered wounds, guilt, and pain will involve discussions with God about the goals and purpose He still has for our life. Too many people hunker down into a hole permanently whenever injustice and selfish people derail their plans. Those who conquer the evil in their world start creating new goals and aim at new mountains to climb, and as a result, they move past the emotional and mental prisons that others want to capture them in. It is surely the plans of the Devil to get us to wallow in our pain, guilt, and difficulties—to give up on the righteousness that we could accomplish in the world. Most people need to work out with God why they are here on earth and what the weekly, monthly, yearly, and long-term goals are for their life. This all takes discussions with God, since He is the only one who truly knows us and knows what our future holds. Two great verses to start with are:

> *"For I know the plans that I have for you,' declares the Lord, 'plans for welfare and not for calamity to give you a future and a hope."* *(Jer 29:11)*

> *"And we know that God causes all things to work together for good to those who love God, to those who are called according to His purpose."* *(Rom 8:28)*

Put simply, we are here for a reason, put here by God to carry out His purposes through us. His plans for us will be for our welfare and our good, not calamity or destruction. Our future is one of hope and promise. We will only overcome the slights that barge into our lives by working toward our goals and a sense of destiny.

Below are some questions for you to think through and answer, perhaps in a journal or even just talk over with another person. If you've never asked these questions and allowed yourself the time to commit to honest answers, this is as good a time as any. Answer the following questions:

> *"Why are you here?"*

> *"What is your purpose in life?"*

We all have a purpose and God has a way for us to fulfill that purpose even if we have messed up in the past. One of the most liberating discussions that people have with themselves and with God is about getting back to what they were put on this earth to do. There are many different righteous pathways and purposes. All are needed to have a society that functions well and provides opportunities of others. Read Ephesians 2:10, "For we are His workmanship, created in Christ Jesus for good works, which God prepared beforehand so that we would walk in them." Let these words sink in and ask yourself, "*What are your goals?*"

It is only when you are headed to a positive place that you can truly move beyond the negativity of the past. Writing out your goals and talking with God about them on a regular basis will cause you to see how to accomplish them in ways you never considered. God moves to help you accomplish your righteous goals, as Jesus says, "Blessed are those who hunger and thirst after righteousness for they shall be satisfied." (Matt 5:6)

Other questions to think about:

"*What are you good at?*"

"*What are the ways that you make a positive difference in the lives of others?*"

"*What brings you righteous joy and delight?*"

"*What do you want to be remembered for?*"

I hope you will take some time to truly put thought, prayer, and pen to action when answering these questions. Focus on this exercise and allow your past to be in your past, and your future to be one of hope and promise.

5. Letting God love us and allowing His love to flow through us in more powerful and very specific ways.

Another exercise that is crucial in recovery from deep wounds and pain is the ability to let love flow through you to others. Many times, because of wounds, guilt, or pain, we are not open to new relationships or new opportunities that are bringing the love of God to us. We must have discussions with God about what we need to be open to and who we need to spread His love out toward. I have found most people need to have these types of discussions constantly, as each day brings new ways to experience the love of God and to spread His love to others.

Since we know that God loves us and wants to manifest His love to us, we can be confident that God's love is streaming toward us even if we are so emotionally distraught we cannot perceive it. We need to talk with God, asking *"How are you trying to get your love to me?"* Pause and let Him show you the ways that He is right now loving you. *"Who are you sending to manifest your love to me?"* Pause and let God bring different people to mind who have been trying to care for you in different ways. *"What have I been unwilling to consider that may be your love coming toward me?"*

We cannot just be a big reservoir where love flows in but does not flow out. God wants you to be His agent doing kind, helpful, loving things for others. Ask Him, *"Who do you want me to love today, Lord?" "What needs can I meet in others today?"* Have an active dialogue with the living God about where, how, and who He wants His love to be shared with. When we finally begin to escape the gravity of our own self-focus, that is the point where we can recover from our lack, pain, wounds, and hurts.

6. **Finding peace.**

Finally, most people need to have constant discussions about bringing peace to their lives if they are to move on from bitterness. When you are no longer plagued by wounds, guilt, and pain, you have peace in your life. This means that you must start building peace in your life even while you are still not done with the wounds, guilt, and pain. Peace is the combination of harmony with others, order in your life, and calm reactions to the events of life. I find that I need to constantly have dialogues with God about these issues so that my forgiveness is not jeopardized by circumstances.

Use these prayer exercises to stretch your mind and actions towards peace.

Exercise #1—*"What would I have to do to live in harmony with this person that I am right now at war with?"* If the answer is doable and does not involve immorality, illegality, or a loss of personhood, then have a long discussion with God about whether He wants you to move into a new harmony with this person.

Exercise #2—*"If I were to bring order to my life so it is less chaotic and arbitrary, what would I need to do?"* Too many of us allow the wreckage of the past to remain in our life by not cleaning up the mess or changing the routines that have developed because of the damage. Start anew and build a life based upon order, schedule, discipline, and an absence of clutter. Remove the clutter of the past, or ask someone else to help you remove it. It is often impossible to move on until the clutter is gone.

Exercise #3—*"What needs to be different in order to have peace in my life?"* If your children must behave in a new way or at a new level in order for there to be peace, then look for how that can happen. If your spouse needs to be sensitive in new ways, then have those discussions about what that looks like. If new activities suddenly sound interesting, then explore them (as long as they are not immoral or lead to immorality). If your career must be different because of what you have been through, then don't just try and soldier on because you always have in the past. Start outlining what type of career changes you would need to make for life to work in your new reality. Don't just keep doing something after it is clear that it is not working. All of these things are subjects to discuss with God in your moving forward with forgiveness. The end goal of forgiveness is a life of peace.

Exercise #4—*"What types of calm are needed in your life from yourself, others, or your environment in order for there to be peace in your life?"* God has told us that the fruit of the Spirit is peace. (Gal 5:22-23) Our lives need to be constantly moving toward a reflection of the harmony, order, and calm that comes from the Holy Spirit. What would it take to get there? What would you need to add to your schedule? What would you need to eliminate?

At times, we will find ourselves overwhelmed by bitterness, guilt, condemnation, and anger, and we need to practice the prayer exercises of forgiveness to keep from being spoiled by the sinfulness inside us and all around us. I hope you can see that each of Jesus' statements in this model prayer are doorways into vast discussions with God about core ideas in life.

In the Appendix "The Radical Power of Forgiveness," I have listed various Scriptures that are a part of the forgiveness process. Go to that section of the book and discuss with God about how to do these in your life. It is the discussion with God and your acting on Scripture that produces the great prayer life with God. Enjoy!

7.

GOD, HELP ME AVOID TRIALS, TESTS, AND TEMPTATIONS!

"And do not lead us into temptation." *(Matt 6:13a)*

T HIS BOOK IS HOPEFULLY TEACHING THAT EACH SENTENCE IN THE LORD'S PRAYER IS AN invitation to have a dialogue with God about the core things of life. Each one has one or more prayer exercises to deepen your walk with God and open up a back-and-forth discussion. The Lord's Prayer is Jesus' instruction for His disciples in the art of conversation with God, pointing out the things that we should engage Him in when we pray. In Luke 11, we might remember that the disciples had just finished watching Jesus have an amazing, interactive, and intimate dialogue with God the Father and the Holy Spirit. They asked Jesus if He would teach them how to pray the way He does so that they, too, could have that kind of relationship with God.

What I think is awesome is that Jesus did not discount their request; He did not say that it was not possible for them as mere men to have that level of relationship He has with God the Father and the Holy Spirit. Instead, He told them (and us) that there are key topics and conversations to constantly have with God that will develop into the real, intimate relationship they (we) desire. As a man, Jesus is the perfect role model to help us enter into the most wonderful and powerful relationship of all. This relationship is available to everyone through Jesus' life, death, resurrection, and teachings. It is a shame that so many miss it and just recite words on a page.

Our Father who is in heaven,

Hallowed be Your Name;

Your Kingdom come;

Your Will be done on earth as it is in heaven;

Give us this day our daily bread;

Forgive us our debts, as we also have forgiven our debtors;

And do not lead us into temptation;

But deliver us from evil.

For Yours is the kingdom and the power and the glory forever. Amen.

The seventh statement is rather shocking when you understand what Jesus meant when He said the words "Lead us not into temptation." His instruction tells us we will need to have many conversations with God about the spiritual battles going on throughout our life, even daily. Our life is not set in stone with certain trials predestined to occur. Our interactive, devotional life with God can change the course of our life. Do you know what this means? It means we can miss certain trials. We can be spared certain temptations. We can initiate opt-out possibilities in regard to tests, trials, and temptations. This critical sentence sends our minds spinning with possibilities!

We see Jesus having many of these types of spiritual-warfare conversations with His disciples and in His prayer life with God the Father. He modeled it for us in many places throughout Scripture. Remember, each one of these sentences is not a magic phrase, but a guide to dialogue and expand conversations with God. Jesus, Himself, had many of these types of spiritual-warfare conversations with His disciples and the Father throughout His ministry. Let me show you some of these verses:

"Then Jesus was led up by the Spirit into the wilderness to be tempted by the devil." (Matt 4:1)

"And do not lead us into temptation, but deliver us from evil. For Yours is the kingdom and the power and the glory forever. Amen." (Matt 6:12)

"And He went a little beyond them, and fell on His face and prayed, saying, 'My Father, if it is possible, let this cup pass from Me; yet not as I will, but as You will.'" (Matt 26:39)

"When He arrived at the place, He said to them, 'Pray that you may not enter into temptation.'" (Luke 22:40)

"No temptation has overtaken you but such as is common to man; and God is faithful, who will not allow you to be tempted beyond what you are

able, but with the temptation will provide the way of escape also, so that you will be able to endure it." (1 Cor 10:13)

"Consider it all joy, my brethren, when you encounter various trials, knowing that the testing of your faith produces endurance." (Jas 1:2,3)

"You meant it for evil but God meant it for good to bring about this present result." (Gen 50:20)

I hope it is clear from the variety of these verses and the spiritual giants who say them that you and I also need to have spiritual-warfare conversations with God about our life. These talks with God will help us to understand what is happening to us and against us within the context of spiritual warfare. Jesus understood this and knew that we would need to ask God for all the help here. The good news is that we don't have to be victims or passive participants enduring an endless stream of difficulties. We can, instead, receive the warnings and take the ways of escape that God provides—all given to us when we talk with God and He talks back.

So how do we do that?

Let's begin by interacting with God when we begin to face testing and trials. Here's an example of what this might look like. I can imagine a conversation like this one, *"Dear Lord, my job has asked me to handle this new area that I do not feel I am really skilled at or want to become skilled at. This is a clearly a test, and I want to stay doing what I am doing now. Lord, do I need to take this assignment? What do you want me to learn by doing that assignment? I would like to be reassigned to this other area rather than this area.*

I cannot see the value in my allowing this transfer to take place."

As the Lord brings ideas and verses to your mind, you continue the dialogue and press the case of missing that assignment at work. Many more dialogues continue while you are at work and your bosses decide if you will be transferred to this new department. Keep praying and be ready to receive the answer from God whether you have been let out of the assignment or the answer is, *"No, you need to go through this trial to grow you."* We also need to be aware of what is going on around us and against us within the context of spiritual warfare. You'll want to pray, *"Lord, I believe that one of my co-workers is being flirtatious, meaning that I need to shut that temptation down in the best possible way. I have also noticed that there are opportunities to gossip and even slander others, and I am so tempted to get sucked into those discussions that put down other people. Please show me how I can pass out of that temptation and not get drawn into these entanglements."*

This interaction with God will go back and forth as He brings to mind ways to not see these people or not engage in those conversations or provide things to say to shut down the negative orientations of the conversations. Asking the Lord Jesus to help you avoid the very things He wants you to avoid is the conversation He wants to have. Too often, we want to get as close to sin as possible before we turn away. We enjoy feeling the pull of temptation and do not see the destructiveness of sin. We need to ask God for all the help we can receive, and we need to recognize when our natural tendencies put us in greater peril.

Digging Deeper

Let us deal with the technical ideas for this verse to better understand why Jesus tells us that dialogues like these are so important. There are a number of very interesting words and ideas to explore that might make this clearer.

Lead us not...

When Jesus said "lead us not," He used the Greek phrase *kai me eisenegkeis*, which has been translated mostly as "lead us not," "bring us not," "introduce us not," "to cause someone to be brought into an event or state." This phrase is written in permissive imperative, according to grammarians, so the idea then is: "Do not allow us to be led into temptation." There is a way out (1 Cor 10:13), but it is a terrible risk to get into the place of temptation in the first place.[6] What is clear from all the definitions of this word and uses in Scripture in and around trials, temptations, and testing is that God allows us, even leads us, to be tested, tried, and even tempted. Why? In order to make us stronger; He wants to lock in the progress that we have made in maturity and to qualify us for the next level of blessing. It's an opportunity for us to prove that we will not fall away from the righteous path we have chosen when the heat is turned up in our life. God has a purpose in it.

into temptation...

The key word in this whole spiritual exercise is the word translated here as *temptation*. It is the Greek word *perismos*, which means trial, test, temptation, or difficulty. The meaning of the words specifically is determined by the context. It is instructive to realize that the three different

---

6 Robertson, A. T. (1933). *Word Pictures in the New Testament, Matthew 6:13.* (Nashville, TN: Broadman Press).

ideas—test, trial, and temptation—come together in this word. It is often helpful to translate this word as "test" so that the negative connotation of temptation does not twist our understanding about a verse before we ever begin thinking about it.

With this understanding, then, Jesus' instruction would read, "*Lead us not into testing, but deliver us from evil.*" This suggests that Jesus wants us to have a dialogue with God about the kinds of tests, trials, and temptations that could come our way over the next few days. We might ask God, *"Are there areas coming where I could have difficulty or stray from the path of the righteous? Where am I right now already facing affliction, opposition, and temptation? Is there a person who is sexually tempting? Are there opportunities to steal or defraud? Are gossip, slander, and negativity rampant? Are pride, ego, arrogance, and bigotry swirling in the conversations near me? Are certain sins excused with some of the people I am hanging around with?"* There are certain tests, trials, and temptations that would defeat us if we allow them to work on us. We need to be somewhere else. Jesus says that through our discussions with God, we can prepare for them, bypass out of some of them, and grow up before some of them even occur. They just aren't necessary any more.

In the case of Peter in Mark 14:27–31, Jesus was trying to help Peter avoid one of his greatest defeats during the time of Jesus' arrest—denying Christ. If Peter had only been less impetuous and not pushed into the palace of the high priest, he would not have been sucked into the scene where he denied Christ a number of times.[7] Peter ignored Jesus' prophetic warning and plunged into the greatest

---

7Jamieson, R., Fausset, A. R., & Brown, D. (1997). *Commentary Critical and Explanatory on the Whole Bible, Vol. 2.* (Oak Harbor, WA: Logos Research Systems, Inc.), 27.

regret of his life. Jesus probably wanted Peter to dialogue with Him about what was coming and how to avoid it, but Peter brushed off his own weaknesses as though they were not there. When was the last time you had an extended dialogue with God in prayer about the person who bugs you or the assignment that doesn't seem fair or the temptation that keeps grabbing your interest? This type of prayer dialogue is extremely important to your future. You can be proactive. God offers ways of escape and strength that will move you significantly forward.

As humans, we see the "test," "trial," and "temptation" in stark contrast. A trial is different than a temptation, because we may have caused the trial, but we think of a temptation as something coming at us to harm us. A test comes to us to train us or qualify us, different from a temptation, which is designed to cause us to fail. What seems to be true scripturally is that a difficulty or obstacle could be seen as a trial or a test or a temptation depending on the point of view. Just as Joseph's being sold into slavery in Egypt was a trial initiated by his brothers and something the Devil used to tempt Joseph to give into despair and immoral choices, it was also used as a test by God. Joseph saw this, and in Genesis 50:20, says to his brothers, "You meant it for evil but God meant it for good to bring about this present result."

First Corinthians 10:13 says, "No temptation has overtaken you but such as is common to man, and God is faithful, who will not allow you to be tempted beyond what you are able, but with the temptation will provide a way of escape also, so that you may be able to endure it." It is the same word *perisomos* translated as temptation. In other words, when we face a difficulty, it is often all three—a trial, a test, and a temptation. Now let me be clear that God never *brings* a temptation. (Jas 1:13) Many times, our own choices and actions put us in a place where the Devil asks for the right to sift us as wheat (Luke 22:31) or attack us (Job 1). God's design is a test meant to move you to the next level of spiritual development (Job 42:5, 6), and He has allowed the Devil to administer the test. In a certain sense, it is our response to this difficulty that determines what it becomes to us. Will it become a trial, a test, or temptation? It depends on how we interact with it.

This idea of testing, trials, and temptations is really one big jumble of issues that will come into our lives, and knowing that this really means *testing* helps us see certain key verses clearly. For example, in James 1:2, 3, it would read, *"Consider it all joy, my brothers, when you encounter various **tests** knowing that the **testing** of your faith produces endurance."* In 1 Corinthians 10:13, it would read, *"No **testing** has overtaken you but such as is common to man, and with the **testing,** God will provide a way of escape that you may be able to endure it."* The book of Job reminds us that *"man is born for trouble as surely as sparks fly upward."* (Job 5:7) God has placed us in a world that is not heaven. The perfect world has not yet arrived. Fortunately, we are in a good world where the law of reaping and sowing is still in effect (Gal 6:7), but we will be tested, tried, and even tempted to see if we will stay on the path of righteousness.

Let's look at this very practically. If you have a very challenging issue going on in your life right now, ask the Lord, *"Is there any way that I caused or drew this difficulty into my life?"* That is a dialogue worth having. The people around us can see that we create our problems through how we act, but we are often so blinded. God wants to talk about this with you. Our problems repeat because we have not grown enough so as to repel and avoid certain problems. We haven't passed the test.

So often we see a problem where God is sending an opportunity. I have found that people can get locked into a way of seeing a person or a situation and they cannot get free until they start using a different metaphor to explain the situation. They see a person as always opposing them because their requests receive a "no," but if the person is approached as a mentor or coach, then the picture changes. God will lead you to dialogues with others out of your dialogues with Him. Only as you see the problems and issues differently will the path to growth and joy become obvious.

Our choices, using the wisdom, mercy, and grace of God, allows us to be invested in the life God gives as though we have won it. Embrace the life God has given you with all the power and love He gives you. Overcome all the obstacles and win the righteous life that God has planned for you. Pass the tests.

What is clear from Scripture and every biblical character is that God uses situations, events, relationships, finances, and vocational issues to present choices to everyone. God brought difficulty, trials, obstacles, and choices to Abraham, Jacob, Rebekah, Esau, Joseph, Moses, Aaron, Samuel, David, Peter, Paul, Barnabas, and even Jesus Himself. God matures us through our choices. God qualifies us through choices. It is our choices that determine the direction of our lives. God even disqualifies us through choices at times. God repeats choices. This is what He does. How we respond to those opportunities and choices determines what comes next.

Modeling Jesus' Prayer

In one of the most amazing scenes in all of the Scriptures, Jesus, the Son of God, asks God the Father if the opportunity to save mankind can be done in some other way. He did not want to go through what He was about to go through, a very painful, humiliating death on a cross. (Matt 26:39) When the answer came back that there was no other way, Jesus submitted and willingly endured the physical, emotional, and spiritual brutality of the cross, carrying the spiritual weight of the sins of the world throughout the ordeal. Jesus, in this prayer in the garden of Gethsemane, did what He instructs us to do in this model prayer. He had a dialogue with the Father about the spiritual warfare that He was about to enter. "Can I get out of this?" or "Can we do it some other way?" He asked.

That this model prayer compels believers to regularly have discussions with God on what to do about the tests, trials, and temptations that are surely coming is significant. I have made this type of dialogue a regular part of my own discussions with God each night, and I have shared my methodology in Exercise #1 below. Just like Peter should have changed his approach the evening of Christ's arrest, we too need to be open to the whispers of the Holy Spirit through the Word of God to change our approach to our days.

What if we began having honest conversations with God about the tests that we are going through? Talk with God about the fear, the doubt, the difficulty, the anger, and even the unfair nature of the trial. Talk about how you want to get out of the trial. Talk about what God wants you to learn from this difficulty. Have a long interaction about the feelings that are moving you in particular directions, especially the feelings that are seductive, moving you in a bad direction. You have to have this dialogue before you are too blinded by what has happened to move in a new direction.

Exercise #1—Talking with God about possible tests, trials, and temptations
The way that I work through this topic in my prayer life with God is by seeking the answer to the question, *"Where am I going to face testing, trials, or temptation today or tomorrow, and how do I avoid it?"* I do this prayer nightly as I contemplate my schedule for the next day. I ask God to show me from His Word what I need to be ready for, alert to, or avoid. I slowly read the chapter of Proverbs for that day (if the next day will be the 13th of the month, then I read the 13th Proverb) to see if any of the verses stand out to me or connect with one of my meetings, appointments, or work periods for the next day. I am amazed at how I always find one verse that stands out and speaks to the coming events. It sensitizes me to the tests, trials, and temptations that could come my way. I have an answer. I am ready.

Just last night I was praying through Proverbs 13 and the verse, *"He who guards his lips preserves his life, and he who opens wide his lips comes to ruin."* I knew then that I would face an opportunity to say too much in one of my many meetings or interactions the next day. I was ready. I was prepared.

There are other times I go to the Psalm for the next day (13, 43, 73, 103, 133) and look for insights and wisdom I might need. Others times I sense that God wants me to study a particular character of the Bible like Barnabas, Obadiah, Ahithophel, Deborah, and so on. There are times when I just pour through the gospels seeking God's wisdom. I often land in Philippians or James for straight advice on how to handle difficult situations. I think about my concerns and problems, asking God for wisdom. God will always have a verse stand out which deals with those very issues, people, or difficulties. I am absolutely amazed about how this simple exercise brings about wisdom, preparation, and even changes to my schedule for the next day. I know that I have escaped many disasters by using this method.

Exercise #2—Identifying the test
How many of you have ever had to take a test or pass an interview to get a job you wanted? Well, God is also in the business of giving us a test before He puts the next level of blessings upon us. He calls them tests and trials, and sometimes He allows the Devil to administrate them. God is hoping you pass; the Devil is trying to get you to fail. If you doubt this, read Job 1.

God regularly wants to bless us in the following relational arenas, but He usually precedes His blessings with a test or a trial. That is why the apostle James says, *"Consider it all joy my brethren when you encounter various trials knowing that the testing of your faith produces endurance, and let endurance have its perfect result that you may be perfect and complete, lacking in nothing...Every perfect gift comes from above from the Father of lights from whom there is no darkness or shadow caused by turning."* (James 1:2-4;17)

I have found that the tests come through the following list of relational categories. Sometimes it is more than one relational category, but usually not all.

Category:	Relationship:	Question to Ask:
Spirituality	Between you and God	*"How am I being tested, tried, or tempted in my relationship with God?"*
Personal Development	Your mental, spiritual, emotional, and physical aspects	*"How am I being tested, tried, or tempted in my relationship with myself?"*
Marital/ Romantic	With your spouse or romantic interest	*"How am I being tested, tried, or tempted in relationship with my spouse or girlfriend/ boyfriend, or as a single person?"*
Family	With your family, both immediate and extended	*"How am I being tested, tried, or tempted relationship with my family?"*

Category:	Relationship:	Question to Ask:
Work	With your work, businesses, bosses, colleagues, and subordinates	*"How am I being tested, tried, or tempted at work?"*
Church	With your church and/or support system	*"How am I being tested, tried, or tempted at church?"*
Money	With money, trying not to have it become a god or idol, generosity	*"How am I being tested, tried, or tempted in finances?"*
Friends	With your friends.	*"How am I being tested, tried, or tempted with friends?"*
Society	With your community, region, and nation	*"How am I being tested, tried, or tempted with society?"*

Category:	Relationship:	Question to Ask:
Enemies	With those who oppose you or are rivals	*"How am I being tested, tried, or tempted with enemies?"*

God wants us to move us forward in each of these relationships. He must test and train us in them before He blesses us with the new responsibilities, opportunities, or the relationships we desire. In which of the above are you facing a good deal of conflict, tension, fear, or set back? It is these areas where you need to look for the test, the trial.

What is God trying to teach?

What do you need to learn?

What wisdom do you need that will allow you to pass out of that test?

Exercise #3—Passing the tests for advancement

God wants to bless us, but in many ways, we don't want to learn and grow. What is it that we have to do or how do we have to act like in order to be able to pass out of this test or trial? This is often all we think about. When I was in college and graduate school, I faced many tests and challenges. But one in particular stands out to illustrate my point on this topic. Entering graduate school, we could challenge a class so that we did not have to take the whole class. You had to take a test designed by the professor of the course to prove that you knew the material of that class so well that it was clear that you did not need to take that class.

I remember challenging the first-year Greek class so that I would not have to pay for that class. I had taken a wonderful correspondence class in New Testament Greek and thought I had the skills to skip this basic class. Passing meant that I would be allowed to go right into the more advanced Greek class working on various portions of the New Testament. I remember the day of the test—the day I would see if I was going to be allowed to skip "baby" Greek. I was very nervous and I had reviewed all my notes and texts from the course I had already taken. I was given the exam and spent over an hour and a half sweating over words, definitions, translations, and grammar. It was quite an ordeal.

The next week, I received back the news that I had passed the test and would be able to enroll in the more advanced Greek course at the seminary. I was excited because I didn't have to spend the money. I didn't have to waste the time on things I already knew. I felt like a big shot, up until I got into the Greek class that I qualified for and realized that there was an awful lot I did not know about Greek! I had passed out of one test and enrolled in another level of training.

In much the same way, God runs tests to see if we are ready for the next level of relationships and responsibility. If you pass, then you move on. If you don't pass, then the course repeats until you pass the test or just get completely stuck at a particular level. God is sending us various situations, people, and challenges to stretch, grow, and give you feedback. Can you handle this particular type of situation? When you can handle a particular situation or type of person, then you are presented with the next level of issues, problems, and challenges. There is no reason to stay stuck where you are. Grow and you will begin advancing in opportunities, challenges, and responsibilities.

Jesus is asking us to ask the Father if we can pass out of certain tests that He knows we will pass. Can we just be promoted because of what we have already been through? Is there another way?

What kind of conversation are you going to have with God about the various arenas of life and the trials taking place in them? I just finished a grueling trial and training period in my work arena where I was learning all I could, trying new things, fighting off fears that I would fail, growing in humility and ability, and enduring slings and arrows from people who did not understand my situation. But I just heard that I passed and the dilemma that I faced is now over. Praise God! God says I have passed. I have grown. I have persevered. I do not want to ever go through that kind of test again, but it did change me in profound ways. It made me a better person, a better Christian, and a better leader. I am interested in what I am now qualified to do in God's service because of it.

Have the deep conversation with God about what is going on in the tests, trials, and temptations of life. Don't just scream, "Get me out of this!" Ask the questions,

"Why is this in my life?"

"Can I do anything different to eliminate this?"

"What do I need to learn, decide, or do that will allow me to graduate from this?"

"What is God up to and how do I cooperate with His purpose?"

"Why am I so tempted by this clearly wrong thing?"

"How do I protect myself from giving in on this issue?"

"How do I recover from failing the test and/or temptation?"

All of these and many more should be a part of your constant dialogue with God so that you can do as Moses tells us, *"present to God a heart of wisdom at the end of our days."* (Psalm 90:12)

Next, we will discuss a topic that many Christians don't want to acknowledge or believe they are immune to just because they are Christians. Evil is biblical and present today. Jesus seems to think it's important and tells us to talk to God about it regularly. Let's read on.

8.

GOD, HELP ME AVOID EVIL!

"...but deliver us from evil." (Matt 6:13b)

J ESUS ADDS A SMALL, FIVE-LETTER POSTSCRIPT
TO THE PRAYER DISCUSSION ON LEAD US NOT
into temptation that we would think does not need to be
said but it was. And so, we are intrigued by Jesus' inclusion
of it. Most of us think that belief in God automatically
enrolls us in the "delivered from evil" group. But both
reality and this hint teaches us differently. Remember
that Jesus is not giving us the specific words to pray but
is suggesting topics to dialogue with God about that are
important to Him—things He knows we will need in this
life to prosper righteously.

The classic definition of evil is something that causes
harm. From a Christian perspective, we are supposed to
pursue the benefit of oneself and others. This is called
doing good. But evil is when one causes harm to others
either directly or in pursuing good for oneself at the
expense of others. Evil began in God's good universe when

a very powerful angel, who moved selfishly beyond his assigned station for personal gain, corrupted one third of the angelic realm to rebel against God. (Ezek 28:12–19; Isa 14:12–15) Evil was further introduced into our world through the corruption of Adam and Eve and their selfish choice to become their own gods by determining their own definitions of good and evil. After Adam and Eve, we were all born into a corrupted state in which our default setting was selfishness. "I want what I want" is the dominant impulse within us. It is through parenting, learning, faith, and social interaction that we are supposed to learn to corral our normal selfishness and favor our positive and beneficial impulses. If we are consistently or egregiously harming others, we will be labeled as evil and punished in various ways in society.

The Ten Commandments

Jesus says that we should have a dialogue with God about being delivered from evil. There will be options and possibilities that present themselves to us on a daily basis that may give significant gains to us but will wound, harm, or destroy other people. This is what we should avoid and be delivered from. God has already given us a cheat sheet to know what those actions look like so we can avoid them. It is called the Ten Commandments. Each of these commandments is a win-lose red line for relating to others. If I steal or lie to get what I need or want, then I am harming others. If I refuse to take a day off, I harm myself and those who work for me. If I commit adultery or use violence to get my way, then I am clearly harming others. If I verbally abuse others to get my way, I have crossed the win-lose red line. If I scheme to take others people's rightful possessions, then I have become evil. Jesus is anticipating all of these options coming at us, and He wants us to dialogue with God about being delivered from committing evil.

Exercise #1—Pray through the Ten Commandments (Ex 20:1-17)
Praying through the Ten Commandments allows God to show you where you might be moving toward or are already involved in evil. In this exercise, ask for God's deliverance for any areas where you have crossed one of these lines. Also, make definite plans that will move you away from violating any of these crucial issues.

- Thou shall have no other gods before me

- Thou shall not make for yourselves any graven images

- Thou shall not take the name of the Lord your God in vain

- Remember the Sabbath Day

- Honor your Father and your Mother

- You shall not murder

- You shall not commit adultery

- You shall not steal

- You shall not bear false witness against your neighbor

- You shall not covet anything that belongs to your neighbor

The Three Sources of Evil

In various parts of the Bible, the believer is encouraged to be aware of three different sources of evil. (1 John 2:15-18; Gal 5:19-21; Eph 6:10-18) The fact that this sentence "deliver us from evil" is a part of this very short list of prayer topics and spiritual exercises tells us that we need to be vigilant about where evil could come from in our lives. Let's discuss each of these to get a better understanding of what we are dealing with.

First, the world systems, institutions, and cultures that promote certain interests at the expense of certain individuals or groups. The world system in every age wants you to put personal comfort and personal gain above God's values of justice, lovingkindness, and righteousness.

Second, the selfish impulses that arise within us that push for our gain at the expense of others. There is within all of us a natural selfishness that wants more for us, and if others have less, then that is too bad for them. This tendency for selfishness can be quite evil and can permit monstrous things to occur as long as we get ours. This is the source of corruption and injustice in every city.

The third source of evil is the Devil and his demons, who promote various schemes and temptations that promise your gain at the expense of others. The Devil is only too willing to promise all types of rewards and benefits if you will allow or participate in damaging or destroying others.

Exercise #2—Identify the source of evil

We need to pray through these three sources of evil. Jesus tells us to enter into a back-and-forth discussion with God about the presence of evil in your life. In this world, evil is a present reality. Evil does want to destroy your potential. It does want to use you to harm others. It does want to imprison you so that you are unable to be the blessing and benefit to others you could be. Use questions like the following to begin the discussion with God about deliverance from evil.

Lord, I know that evil will always seek to get a hold on my life. In what ways am I being positioned toward evil? Please protect me and show me what I must do to strengthen your deliverance and protection. What is the source of the evil I am currently facing?

Lord, show me how the world is trying to tempt me to evil. How is the lust of the world, the lust of the flesh, and the boastful pride of life seeking to trick me into getting out of God's will and participating in something that will harm others? (1 John 2:15-18)

Lord, show me how my flesh is trying to tempt me to evil. How is my own sinful nature trying to seduce me into selfishness at a level that I become harmful to God or others? Am I being tempted to immorality, impurity, sensuality, idolatry, sorcery, enmities, strife, jealousy, outbursts of anger, disputes, dissensions, factions, envying, drunkenness, or carousing?

Lord, show me how the Devil and his demons are trying to tempt me or move me to evil. Is it through desire, fear, opposition, slander, spiritual power, anger, ego, perversion? These are the major schemes of the Devil.

Lord, show me the opportunities and possibilities that might lead me to harming others.

Lord, show me the evil that is just around the corner seeking to do me harm.

Lord, what do I need to do or ask you for that will deliver me from the evil that I could fall victim to?

Lord, in what ways am I being set up to make it easier to compromise my values at some point down the road?

One of the things that this phrase in the Lord's Prayer suggests is that God wants to engage with you about a subject that most people want to hide from Him. God says, "Let's talk about everything in your life and especially the evil." Are you having a discussion with God about the evil that is being presented to you? Are you having a discussion with God about escaping the evil that is coming at you? Are you listening for the guidance of the Holy Spirit on how to be delivered from the evil that is seeking to do you harm? Begin praying to God about these things right now and see how your mind lights up with the discussion.

Exercise #3—Freedom from worldly evil
If God has disclosed to you that the evil coming at you is sourced in the world, then look to 1 John 2:15-18, God's prescription in regard to the world's allure.

"Do not love the world, nor the things in the world. If anyone loves the world, the love of the Father is not in him. For all that is in the world, the lust of the flesh, the lust of the eyes, and the boastful pride of life is not from the Father but is from the world.

The world is passing away, and also its lusts; but the one who does the will of God lives forever."

The world system and culture wants us to fall for the fads and values of the peer group around us. It wants us to love (pursue, please, and meet the needs of) the world's ideas and people. It focuses us on what is pleasant and desirable for our body and selfish nature. It wants us to desire whatever looks good to us. It wants us to take great pride in the acclaim of those around us. If we chase those things, then we can be hugely deceived and do monstrous damage to ourselves and others. We do need to be delivered from pursuing, pleasing, and meeting the needs of these people and their goals. We must have the discussion with God about this worldly evil. Read 1 John 2:15–18 again, this time slowly and out loud. What stands out to you as you read through it? Where is God directing you? Pray that God would allow you to be free from this area and how you can make changes in your life.

I have often found that deliverance will come in small but significant choices we make. Not going to a particular activity; backing away from a tight relationship with a particular friend; choosing to go hang out with a good group of people; reading your Bible instead of going to the bar; going to bed instead of staying up and surfing the web; not doing the deal that is shady; living a little slower life; making the healthy choices in food, drink, exercise, and rest. These are good places to start.

Exercise #4—Freedom from selfish evil
If the evil we are facing comes largely from our own natural, selfish nature, then we need to be delivered from

this destructive element within us. Notice what God says about our selfish nature in Galatians 5:19–21.

> *"Now the deeds of the flesh are evident, which are: immorality, impurity, sensuality, idolatry, sorcery, enmities, strife, jealousy, outbursts of anger, disputes, dissensions, factions, envying's, drunkenness, carousing and things like these, of which I forewarn you, just as I have forewarned you, that those who practice such things will not inherit the kingdom of God."*

Have the discussion with God about the above tendencies that may be showing up in your life. Are you being pulled toward sensuality? Is there a greater willingness to anger and arguments with others? Do you find that you are seeking solace in drink or food rather than Jesus? Are you enjoying the parties and fast-paced life, skipping the contemplative parts of your life? While it is not evil to have fun, giving into the desire for constant excitement and selfish excess will certainly damage yourself and others.

I have often found that to be delivered from sins of the flesh requires a Christian to die to the sin and become alive to God in some way. You do this by substituting the old action or thought pattern with a different pattern. Notice what Romans 6:11 says, *"Even so consider yourselves dead to sin but alive to God in Christ Jesus."* Die to the thinking about the expression of the desire. Die to doing what you know feeds the wrong desire. Ask God to give you a new thought, a new action, a new activity to substitute in the place of the old pattern. God will bring new ideas, new people, and new choices to mind, and if you do them, you will be delivered from the old, evil patterns. I do find that many people want to be delivered from the old desire but that is not usually what God does. He delivers us from the evil by having us begin living on a completely new path. The old desire is still there if you hang around your old activating patterns and people.

There is such power in talking with the Lord Jesus about your life and seductions and desires you feel. "O Lord, search me and know my heart; Try me and know my anxious thoughts; And see if there be any hurtful way in me and lead me in the way everlasting." (Psalm 139:23,24) Go through the list in Galatians 5:19-21 and see if God is highlighting particular desires and tendencies. Have the right discussions with God and receive His deliverance from evil. Let Him refine you so that He can use you more and bless you further.

Exercise #5—Freedom from the Devil's attack by putting on the Armor of God

There are various ways that God can shield us from evil. If the evil is sourced in the Devil, then we need to look at the Armor of God passage and have a discussion with God about these vital protection pieces. Look at this powerful passage on the Armor of God in Ephesians 6:10-18.

> *"Finally, be strong in the Lord and in his mighty power. Put on the full armor of God, so that you can take your stand against the devil's schemes. For our struggle is not against flesh and blood, but against the rulers, against the authorities, against the powers of this dark world and against the spiritual forces of evil in the heavenly realms. Therefore, put on the full armor of God, so that when the day of evil comes, you may be able to stand your ground,*

and after you have done everything, to stand. Stand firm then, with the belt of truth buckled around your waist, with the breastplate of righteousness in place, and with your feet fitted with the readiness that comes from the gospel of peace. In addition to all this, take up the shield of faith, with which you can extinguish all the flaming arrows of the evil one. Take the helmet of salvation and the sword of the Spirit, which is the word of God. And pray in the Spirit on all occasions with all kinds of prayers and requests. With this in mind, be alert and always keep on praying for all the Lord's people."

There is great value in going over the pieces of the Armor with God and how they need to be applied in your life at a particular time. I encourage people to realize that the Armor of God is not belts, buckles, and swords, but instead Truth, Righteousness, Peace, Faith, Salvation, the Word of God, Prayer, and Alertness. This is a list of very powerful spiritual weapons that can keep you from being damaged or destroyed by the evil one. Discuss with God each of these pieces and let Him bring to mind things that you have not been paying attention to. The Devil comes at us with fear, doubt, bitterness, hatred, shame, and many other vicious emotional weapons. We need to calmly go over with the Lord Jesus His list of protection.

Start by praying something like this,

Dear Lord, I am in a spiritual battle to establish your principles, your values in my life. Show me the pieces of the Armor I have been neglecting or misunderstanding.

Then, go through each piece of armor and ask these types of questions, listening to the still, small voice of God and His instructions.

Truth
What truths do you need to be aware of, learn, or be reminded of in order to be protected against the fear, doubt, anger, bitterness, shame, and hatred that will come at you?

Righteousness
What righteousness of Christ do you need to understand and claim for yourself, and what righteous deeds do you need to personally perform so that you will be protected from the schemes of Satan?

Peace
What elements of peace that Christ has won for believers must you understand in order to let go of fear, doubt, anger, shame, and bitterness? What techniques of peace must you practice to close the doorways of attack from your family, friends, work place, and church?

Faith
What, how, or where is God asking you to trust Him, to have faith that He will keep the enemy from barging into your life and destroying a big part of it?

Salvation
How will God save you in this situation? What ways of escape is God offering? We need to recognize that God sends us convenient and very practical ways of escape.

Word of God

What verses of Scripture keep being brought to mind in the situation you are in? These are often the guidance of the Holy Spirit giving you a sword to plunge into the middle of the Devil's plans for you. Have the discussion with God about the verses you are remembering, being guided toward, or noticing when you read.

Prayer

Pray and seek God's help in the midst of the crisis or difficulty. So often we pray much more fervently when we are in desperate need. Pay attention to what you pray and the thoughts that rush into your mind after you pray. Do new ideas come to you? Do you think of people you could talk to after you pray? Are you aware of new combinations of ideas or new pathways that could be a way out of this dilemma?

Alertness

Finally, discuss with God if this type of crisis has happened in the past. Are you facing a temptation, failing, or weakness that you have faced before? If the answer is yes, ask God and other wise people what you need to put in place so that this issue would be eliminated from your life. Allow yourself to consider solutions and preventative measures that you would not have been willing to consider when you were not in crisis. We often tell ourselves that we can handle a particular temptation that has defeated us before, so we do not put up adequate barriers or warning systems to keep us from falling the next time. Have this discussion with God and put new measures in place.

For a fuller discussion of the Armor of God, see my book *Secrets of the Armor of God,* available online.

Satan's Schemes

Satan has a playbook with specific plays or schemes he runs against us. If the Devil is attacking you, he is most likely attacking you in one of these ways. I use a sort of pull-down menu that opens up my discussions with God about what the Devil is trying against me. This is, what he (the Devil) will try to embroil you in. Knowing the scheme, or play from his playbook, you can prepare yourself to win by praying about how to defeat these various schemes he is running.

Exercise #6—Identifying and praying against Satan's schemes.
Let me take you through a quick understanding of these major schemes. Then have a time of prayer with God about these. Go through each one and have a dialogue with God about whether the Devil is using this one or that one against you and what you should do to prepare for this scheme. Continue the discussion until you have a whole game plan for how you are going to defeat this plan of the Devil. Put on the full armor of God and battle to freedom and victory.

Desire—Tempter
This is the scheme of the Devil as the tempter. In Matthew 4:4, Jesus was led up by the Spirit of God to be tempted by the Devil. In that temptation, the Devil tempted Jesus with food, with power, and with glory. Jesus passed each test by turning away from the desire and staying true to God's plan and timetable. When the Devil comes as tempter, he wants to use a desire in your life to pull you off the straight road. He may use any desire in your world that can derail the plan of God. It could be food, sex, power, popularity, money, comfort, ego, friendship, or a hundred other

139

There is often nothing wrong with the desire that ̶ is using in certain situations, but it is wrong at the ̶̶̶e or in the way that it is being used on you.

Pray, "*Dear Lord, is the Devil scheming against me through temptation or desire?*" Pause and see if the Lord brings situations or temptations to mind. If God does bring things to mind, then ask Him how you can prepare to defeat this scheme? Are there permanent solutions that God wants you to put in place that will keep you from giving into this temptation in the future? If temptation is an issue for you, my book *Mission Possible—Winning the Battle over Temptation* is available to you with forty or so practical ways to defeat temptation. You can also take a video course, which can be accessed through the Principles to Live By website, www.ptlb.com/mission-possible.

Opponent—Satan

This is the scheme of Satan where he lives up to that name. The name "Satan" means adversary – opponent. In this scheme, he will oppose you and come against you as you try and do something good for God. The opposition may come through a person, an institution, a group, or directly. It will be there to move you off the plan you are pursuing for and with God. Do not be moved from what God has planned to accomplish. That is how you win.

Pray, "*Dear Lord, is the Devil scheming against me as Satan, where he will oppose me and seek to destroy me so I cannot accomplish your will for my life?*" Pause and see if God brings up any ways that Satan is coming against you as opponent or adversary. If God brings situations, people, institutions, or groups to mind, then talk about that with the Lord and how you can keep pressing forward or win them to God's point of view. Then talk about how you can continue to move forward in spite of the Devil's opposition. Is there something you need to learn or develop, or are there people you need to reach out to in order to get around this opposition?

Accuser—Devil

This is the scheme of the Devil where he really is a devil. The word "devil" means double-tongued or forked tongue. This scheme is where he spreads rumors, gossip, slander, and accusations. He is trying to get you to move off of the path that you are on and onto a path of revenge and anger. This is often a refining path in which all kinds of things are said about you that are not true. You can answer truthfully, but it doesn't always stop the attack.

Pray, *"Dear Lord, is the Devil coming against me as a devil, an accuser?"* Pause and see if the Lord brings situations, comments, or people to mind who fit this description of this scheme. If the Lord brings things to mind, then have a discussion with Him about how to protect yourself and what He wants you to do to win against this scheme.

Fear—Roaring Lion

This scheme of the Devil is when he becomes the roaring lion using fear to drive you away from something good and positive. Fear can be a debilitating emotion. We want to move away from the source of the fear, yet often that is exactly the opposite thing that God wants you to do. The Devil comes as a roaring lion to roar at you so you'll leave where you should stay in order to get you to move in the opposite direction of where you should be going. In the wild, a lion will roar when it is trying to drive a gazelle toward the real hunters. It is counter intuitive, but the gazelles should run *toward* the sound of the roar because that is the escape route. Dig into 1 Peter 5:8 and see how the roaring lion wants to devour you and not have you make the impact for God you could make.

Pray, *"Dear Lord, is the Devil planning to or is right now the one producing fear in my life to get me to move away from the place where you want me?"* Pause and see if the Lord brings people, places, work, and organizations to mind. If He does, then talk with Him about how you can resist fear by staying put to make more of a positive impact.

Anger / Bitterness—Dragon
This scheme of the Devil is where He comes to make you angry and bitter. He comes as the dragon to fill you with fire that melts the relationships you need with the people that would love you. The dragon scheme is where he gets you to raise your expectations of people to unrealistic levels, or he wants you to nurse bitterness and grievances until you can't stand the very people who may be the keys to your future.

Pray, *"Dear Lord, is the Devil coming against me as a dragon seeking to raise anger and bitterness in my life so that I will not accomplish the work you have for me?"* Pause and see if the Lord brings anything to your mind. If He does, then have a discussion about that person, organization, group, or issue. How does the Lord want you to avoid this scheme? If you have been caught by this scheme, how does He want you to move to freedom and escape the clutches of this scheme?

Spiritual Power—Angel of Light
This is the scheme where the Devil comes as an Angel of Light offering spiritual power or secret revelations that

others do not have. The Devil wants you to be amazed and side-tracked by spiritual nonsense so that you do not pursue the true goals of life (loving God, others, and yourself, righteously). It is always amazing that those who fall for this scheme always end up becoming harmful to others or arrogant and destructive to the relationships they really need.

Pray, *"Dear Lord, is the Devil coming against me as an Angel of Light seeking to deceive me into not building a life of love for You, others, and myself?"* Pause and see if the Lord brings anything person, word, or group to mind. Ask the Lord how you can break free from this deception, and how you can prepare for this scheme the next time.

Perversion—Beelzebub, Prince of Darkness, and the Underworld

This scheme of the Devil is to expose people to the thinking, benefits, and practices of perversion. In this way, he can persuade people get used to wickedness to stay connected to this world. It is the world of gangs, corruption, perverse sexuality, imprisonment, occult rituals, slavery, humiliating power over others, and violence. It seems like it offers lots of benefits initially, even though most realize it is a horrible world to enter. Perversion traps its victims in a dark world where people serve very base and wicked impulses.

Pray, *"Dear Lord, is the Devil coming against me as Beelzebub, seeking to trap me in a world of perversion and wickedness?"* Pause and see if the Lord brings situations, activities, groups, or individuals to mind. Ask God how to break free from this world and to be protected so as not to enter its pathways. Agree with God that participating in this arena is wrong. Plead the death of Christ on the cross to set you free. Find a group of Christians who will pray with you and for you and help you to strengthen your faith in the Lord Jesus through the practice of the spiritual disciplines—and especially reading and studying the Bible.

Pride—God of this world

This is one of the favorite schemes of the Devil, where he wants to increase your own natural self-focus. He wants you to feel justified for making everything about you. He wants you to pursue arrogance, superiority, and ego, and then believe it's okay. Every overbearing leader and bully is caught in this scheme and thinks that he is right. The Devil wants you to believe that you are the god of your world, in complete control and able to treat people poorly because of how important you are. He will inflate your sense of self or the desire for importance.

Pray, *"Dear Lord, is the Devil using pride, ego, importance, or fame as a way to trap me so I don't serve you in some important way?"* Pause and see if God brings some people, some situation, or some boast you made to mind. Ask God how you can break free from this deceptive scheme that seems like you are making progress, but you are really hurting people and missing God's best. For a further discussion of the schemes of the Devil, see my book *Schemes of Satan.*

Who knew that a small five-word postscript at the end of a prayer could have so much packed in to it? Just by mentioning the presence of and deliverance from evil is significant. It is Jesus going straight at a huge issue. He knows that life here on earth is lived in constant danger from evil; He dealt with it personally, numerous times! It is coming at us. It is seeking to corrupt us. We need to be delivered from it. Jesus clearly suggests that we are to be participants in the deliverance that we need. But we need to pray and dialogue with God on a regular basis to do this. I hope this chapter has shown you how.

CONCLUSION

"For Yours is the kingdom and the power and the glory forever. Amen." (Matt 6:13c)

T HROUGHOUT THIS BOOK ABOUT THE LORD'S PRAYER, WE ESSENTIALLY ASKED THE question, "What are the secrets of prayer hidden in this phrase?" We have covered a lot of ground, from finding out what it means to "hallow" God's name, to what it means when we ask for provision. The prayer exercises and dialogues in this unique prayer guide that Jesus gave us has ranged all over and covered many topics that are both specifically about us and specifically about God. But there is one last phrase in this prayer that we must address to help us reach the proper conclusion.

Jesus concludes His most complete discussion of the Lord's Prayer with a doxology that we assume is also a dialogue and not just magic words to say. It should be mentioned that this phrase is included in many versions of the Bible, but not all, and it is not included in the Luke version of the prayer. Scholars believe it is most likely that Jesus repeated this prayer guide on many occasions and this longer ending was included in some, but not all, of the times that He gave this advice on intimacy with God. The gospel writer who heard the longer version included the fullest version, so that we could learn the most. What's really important about this concluding phrase is the hidden secret it contains:

Life is all about God and His purposes.

We must not conclude that a deep relationship with God can be built upon a self-focus, instead of a God-focus. This is what Jesus is guiding us into at the end. Even though I have been praying about myself in a number of the prayer exercises, it has never been about myself. It has been about God's purposes, God's kingdom, and my becoming fit for the highest levels of service, joy, and love within the context of God's plans.

God wants to dialogue with us. He wants us to make progress in relationship with Him, because He knows that the best possible life will be a life abandoned to His purpose for us. (Eph 2:10) Therefore, if you are going to conclude a time of prayer with God Almighty in a way that keeps the relationship growing, then one must remember that we are not in charge, and it is not about us. This prayer time has not been a time of treating God like a genie, where we think we are in charge of this great power and God is waiting to serve us. God is saying YES to us and giving us freely of His blessings and grace, but our requests must be within the boundaries of His preordained plan. God is in charge, and we are serving His kingdom and His purposes. He tells us that if we serve His kingdom, then He will add all we want to us. But we can't start with "what do we want." (Matt 6:33)

It is the Devil who answers prayer meant for purely selfish or evil outcomes. We don't want those to come true. And we should surely not pray those to the Lord God Almighty. In this last part of Jesus' prayer guide, He brings us back to the theme of worship, praise, and acknowledgement of God's position, power, and blessing. God is awesome, and if one is going to have a close relationship with Him, then one needs to be aware of and acknowledge the depth of His being.

So often, we have erected ourselves as our own god, and we are trying to promote our kingdom and purposes. When my wife and I were teaching our children this prayer at the very young ages of three and four, we thought we had helped them memorize it as we regularly said it at the dinner table. Then we had the girls lead us in this prayer, and we found that our middle daughter had adjusted this last line to be a self-proclamation of supremacy. "Mine is the kingdom and the power and glory forever. Amen." Most of humanity is inclined to see it the same way as my daughter did at three years of age. This is exactly why God puts this in the prayer guide that He gave to mankind.

We are trying to fit into God's kingdom plans, not create our own kingdom. We are seeking to connect with, use, and align with God's power, not manipulate His power for our ends. God does love us and has a great plan for our life (Eph 2:10), but we are often so stubborn about pursuing our own plans that we miss His plans for us. Talking with God about His plan, His purposes, His power, and His glory is the exhortation that comes in this last sentence in Jesus' master prayer guide. Have the discussions with God about these issues—His kingdom, His power, His glory—and you will be on your way to seeing the world as it really is and connecting with God in the most positive way.

One of the discussions I have regularly with the Lord is the idea that not everyone is interested in having God's kingdom succeed. I guess I want to believe that everyone will be excited about the rule of righteousness and truth, to understand from reading the Scriptures, with God and reading the news, that the murkiness of this world to hide their ...ess and evil. There are always surprises when ...itical winds shift or economic trends move as parts of people's secret lives and aspirations become known. The Scripture clearly tells us that there will be people who will oppose the coming of God's kingdom. They will not want evil crushed. They will not be interested in righteousness increasing. Significant parts of their fun will be destroyed, and life in a righteous world will be boring, they protest.

Right now, as I write, Western Civilization is trying to find solutions to mankind's problems by asking people who profit by harming others what they think. This will not work, as the wicked will not voluntarily suggest that their gain from damaging others should cease. The kingdom of God does not seek to get everyone to agree and especially not the wicked. We and our culture must come to grips with the fact that in order to install righteousness and truth, those who gain through damaging and destroying others will need to be stopped. God's kingdom is a righteous kingdom. His power moves to redeem the down-trodden and outcast. His glory is expanded through shining a light on darkness and caring for the victims of injustice.

What is the secret of this part of the prayer guide?

In order to have a deep relationship with God, we must be more interested in God's plans than our own. God will not improve status quo, but He will remove those who do evil.

This wonderful passage from Dallas Willard tells of the delight in the Lord's Prayer when we get past just saying it as a memorized prayer. Willard's experience so closely mirrors my experience that I was blown away by the similarity and wanted to include his words here:

"I personally did not find the Lord's Prayer to be the doorway into a praying life until I was in my mid-twenties. In my family, that prayer was, for three generations I know of, always said in unison at the breakfast table. But at some point, for reasons I cannot explain, I began to use it in a new way; taking each phrase of it and slowly and meditatively entering into the depths of its meaning, elaborating within it important details of my current life.

When I began to 'live' in the prayer in this way – for that is the only way I can describe it—there were many nights when I would awaken about two o'clock and spend an hour of delight before God just dwelling in one or more phrases from it. I had to make a point at times, and I still do, of praying thoughtfully through the entire prayer. Otherwise, the riches of one or two phrases in the prayer would be all I could develop, and I would not benefit from all its contents.

Sometimes I do not start at the first request but go immediately to the end or the middle and settle in there for a while. At other times, I will use just the words of the address, 'Our Father filling the heaven,' to establish and reestablish address and orientation as I go through the day."[8]

---

8 Willard, Dallas, *The Divine Conspiracy: Rediscovering Our Hidden Life in God.* (San Francisco: HarperSanFrancisco, 1998), 268.

My deep hope is that you will get involved and do what you can to become the righteous person God desires you to be. It can begin with this book as you use the exercises and keys to dialogue with our great God about your life. Listen for God to talk back as you engage Him on these vital topics. It might take some time and a level of focus you're not used to, but it is worth it. Enjoy!

ACKNOWLEDGMENTS

MANY THANKS TO THE PEOPLE WHO HELPED ME SHAPE THIS BOOK SO IT CONVEYS THE life-changing truths and exercises contained in this prayer guide from Jesus. Let me name just a few that I must thank publicly. To Jennifer Edwards, who did a superb job of editing the various rough drafts so that the concepts are so much clearer and jump into the mind for application. To Kelly Stuber, for her layout and formatting of the content, so that readers engage, keep reading, and try these prayer exercises. To John Chase, for his great creativity in cover design, so that readers want to pick up the book and get started. The men in the Chipotle Bible Study Group, who have tried all the exercises and gave their feedback and insights on how the lessons in this prayer guide helped them, needed updating, allowed them to hear God's voice, and moved them forward spiritually – Scott Hall, Jason Wren, Dr. David Keiner, Bob Sparks, and Joey Petrali. Many thanks, guys; it has been a wonderful ride explaining these concepts and getting your invaluable feedback.

APPENDIX 1:

LEARNING MORE ABOUT PRAYER

THERE ARE SEVERAL KEY THINGS REQUIRED FOR EFFECTIVE PRAYERS—RELATIONSHIP with the Father, faith, and motive of the heart. Prayer is a tricky thing in the church. Everybody says that they pray when a need arises, but few people have actually seen or experienced real, tangible answers. Many people think that their internal selfish desires or wishes for God to act are genuine prayers. Sometimes people wonder why God doesn't do anything in their life. Others want to treat God like a genie in a bottle, summoning Him to grant their selfish wishes, whatever they may be. Prayer is not a magic trick. Yes, He knows everything we are thinking, and we may even, at times, think He has answered something that has been on our minds or in our hearts. But if that is how prayer really worked, then what's the point of having a relationship with God at all? Relationship has to be at the center of answered prayer.

A lot of how we experience the blessings we receive from prayer depends on our current view of prayer—how it works, its effectiveness, its purpose, our own past experiences, and so on. Plus, it depends on our current view of God. Can God really do *anything*? Is He powerful enough? Strong enough? Does He really care? Faith in God and the power of prayer is required. Like Jesus says in Matthew 21:21–22, *"Truly I tell you, if you have faith and do not doubt, not only can you do what was done to the fig tree, but also you can say to this mountain, 'Go, throw yourself into the sea,' and it will be done. If you believe, you will receive whatever you ask for in prayer."* Faith gives us the confidence in God's great power to be able to do anything at any time. The Bible says that faith is the hope for and the assurance of what is not seen. (Heb 11:1) And we know God tenderly cares for us because He says, *"Are not five sparrows sold for two pennies? Yet not one of them is forgotten by God. Indeed, the very hairs of your head are all numbered. Don't be afraid; you are worth more than many sparrows."* (Luke 12:6–7) We know through faith that God cares and that He can.

A huge requirement for effective prayer is motive. For prayer to be effective, we have to get on God's agenda; that is, we need to consider what He wants to do through people like you and me here on earth. God has a list of things He wants to do. He has a number of areas that are of deep interest to Him. And He is waiting to release His power through you in the direction He wants, which Jesus tells us about in the Lord's Prayer.

APPENDIX 2:

EXPLORING THE ATTRIBUTES OF GOD

ANY TIMES, I LOVE TO JUST GO THROUGH THIS LIST OF WHAT IS OFTEN CALLED THE attributes of God and let Him speak to me about how He is all of these things. He will typically focus my mind on one or two particular attributes and let me contemplate the wonder of His being in those ways. For more on this exercise and information about these concepts, see my book *Delighting in God.*

- Infinite—He has no beginning or ending but dwells in eternity which is beyond time, Genesis 21:33

- Self-Existent—He is life in Himself. He does not contain life but is life, Acts 17:24, 25

- Spirit—He is personal, decisive, without a body, and without material substance, 1 Timothy 1:17

- Omniscient—He knows everything and how to do all things for the maximum benefit for all concerned, Isaiah 40:13, 14; Romans 11:33; Psalm 139:1-6

- Omnipotent—God has all power and authority to do whatever He pleases, Psalm 115:3; Revelation 4:11

- Omnipresent—God is present everywhere, Psalm 39:7-12; Proverbs 15:3

- Immutable—The perfections of His nature do not change, Malachi 3:6; Psalm 102:25-27

- Holiness—God is pure; He is not corrupted by sin, selfishness, or a violation of His own perfections; and He can never become corrupted; Psalm 29:2; 1 Peter 1:14-16

- Righteous/Just—He is always right in His decisions, judgments, character, and works, Deuteronomy 32:4; Psalm 19:9

- Goodness—He is the ultimate goal of life. When we seek Him, we will not be disappointed, Psalm 34:8,10; Exodus 33:19

- Longsuffering—He is patient and longsuffering with us, Genesis 6:3; Romans 2:4

- Truth—He is the truth in an ultimate sense that when all is over there will be God, Isaiah 44:8, 9

- Sovereignty—He is in control of the whole of His creation in every way. Nothing happens without His understanding and approval, Daniel 4:35

- Trinity—God describes Himself as Eternal Father, Eternal Son, and Eternal Spirit. He is a Tri-une being, above, and beyond our comprehension. We can grasp the truth of who He is, and we are driven to praise and stand in awe.

APPENDIX 3:

PRAYING THROUGH THE TITLES AND NAMES OF GOD

BECAUSE OF WHAT JESUS CHRIST HAS DONE, YOU ARE ALLOWED TO APPROACH AND interact in a familiar and intimate way the Supreme Being of the Universe, who is all of these things we describe through His names.

- ELOHIM—God as "Creator, Preserver, Transcendent, Mighty, and Strong," Genesis 1:1; 17:7, 6:18, 9:15, 50:24; 1 Kings 8:23

- EL SHADDAI—"God All-Sufficient," Genesis 17:1, 2; The Lord God, the Almighty, Rev 16:7

- ADONAI—"Lord" in our English Bibles. It means that we acknowledge the God of the Bible as our Master and boss. The first uses of Adonai were in Genesis 15:2; 2 Samuel 7:18-22

- YAHWEH—Yahweh is the covenant name of God. From the Hebrew verb "to be," "The Self-Existent One," Exodus 3:14. This could be thought of describing God as the Ever-living One, the One who is life in Himself. He is the great source of all life. This is the personal name of God that He shares with those He invites into covenant with Him.

- YAHWEH-JIREH—"God, the Source of Life, will Provide," Genesis 22:14

- YAHWEH-ROPHE—"God, the Source of Life, who Heals," Exodus 15:22-26

- YAHWEH-M'KADDESH—"God, the Source of Life, who Sanctifies," Leviticus 20:8. "To make whole, set apart for holiness." The idea is that God sets a person apart for His purposes and their highest purpose.

- YAHWEH-SHALOM—"God, the Source of Life, our Peace," Judges 6:24. "Shalom" translated "peace" 170 times means "whole," "finished," "fulfilled." God always brings harmony, beauty, and order out of chaos.

- SHEPHERD—The One who is dedicated to protection, direction, and provision, Psalm 23

- YAHWEH-ROHI—"God, the Source of Life, our Shepherd," Isaiah 40:11

- JUDGE—The One who decides, who passes judgment, who administrates justice, who rules the boundaries of your life. This is shaphat in Hebrew, Psalm 96:13.

- YAHWEH ELOHIM—"God, the Source of Life, who is the Creator, Transcendent, Mighty God," Genesis 2:4

- YAHWEH-TSIDKENU—"God, the Source of Life, who is our Righteousness," Jeremiah 23:5, 6, 33:16. The only reason we have any righteousness before a Holy God is because of what God has done for us and given us.

- YAHWEH-SABAOTH—"God, the Source of Life, who commands all the angelic beings," Isaiah 1:24; 2 Kings 3:9–12

- EL ELYON—"The Most-High God," Genesis 14:18; Deuteronomy 26:19, 32:8; Psalm 18:13. This reference to God was outside the Jewish nation and was what Melchizedek called the God that both He and Abraham worshipped.

- ABHIR—"The Mighty One," Genesis 49:24; Deuteronomy 10:17. God is able to do what is needed in our earthly situations; He is the Mighty One.

- KADOSH—"The Holy God," Psalm 71:22; Isaiah 40:25. God is set apart from sin and is pure. He is also transcendent and completely beyond all of His creatures and creation. When He reveals His Holiness at any level everyone is afraid and proclaims "Holy is the Lord!"

- EL ROI—"The God who Sees," Genesis 16:13. There are times when we think we are forgotten and so far outside of God's will that even He does not notice or care; He is the God who sees and offers us a way back and provision for the journey.

- KANNA EL—"Jealous God," Exodus 20:5, 34:14. God takes pledges of love and obedience seriously. He wants our full attention and devotion. He will not tolerate multiple gods in our life.

- PALET—"Deliverer," Psalm 18:2. God is the one who provides the ultimate way of escape from our sins but also offers us deliverances and ways of escape in the normal course of our life. We get ourselves into bad spots and He provides.

- YESHA—(Y'shua) "Savior," Isaiah 43:3. This is the Hebrew name Joshua which means Savior. God is in so many ways our Savior. So often we want to be our own Savior instead of allowing Him to bring the real redemption our way. Lean into His ways of salvation

- GAOL—"Redeemer," Job 19:25. From one of the earliest sources about mankind's interactions with God, the book of Job, we learn that people called God their redeemer. He would buy them out of the mess they were in and into a new life.

- MAGEN—"Shield," Psalm 3:3, 18:30. We can hide behind God who is our shield when the world around us seeks to beat upon us in ways we cannot handle.

- EL-OLAM—"The God of Everlasting Time," Genesis 21:33; Psalm 90:1-3. He lives outside of time and looks on our lives and our movement through time with complete understanding. Our lives, the history of the world, the existence of our universe is a short length of ribbon on the floor of eternity.

- ZUR—"God our Rock," Deuteronomy 32:18; Isaiah 30:29. The rock was the symbol of stability and security. The rocks had been there for generations and would be there for generations. God could be counted on like the mammoth rocks of Israel.

- Jesus, from the Hebrew "Joshua" meaning JEHOVAH (Yahweh) IS SALVATION. Matthew 1:19-21

- Christ is equivalent to the Hebrew 'Messiah' (Meshiach), "The Anointed One," Matthew 16:13-16

- Bishop and Guardian of our souls—He takes the responsibility to watch over our souls and guard them, 1 Peter 2:25

- Advocate—He is our defense attorney arguing for our acquittal on the basis of His own death in our place, 1 John 2:1, 2

- Propitiation for our sins—He is the full payment for our sins and because of what Jesus did we can stand in the presence of God guilt free, 1 John 2:1, 2

- The Seven-fold Spirit—Spirit of the Lord—Wisdom, Understanding, Counsel, Strength, Knowledge, Fear of the Lord, Spirit of Holiness. The Holy Spirit is called the seven-fold spirit who accomplishes these things in our life as He does His ministry to us and for us, Isaiah 11:1-3. This is the one that you address as Father.

APPENDIX 4:

UNDERSTANDING HOW GOD SEES YOU

WE HAVE MUCH TO BE THANKFUL FOR AS CHILDREN OF GOD. JUST LOOK AT THE rights and privileges we get for aligning ourselves with Christ—the list is extensive! Next time you get down on yourself or feel unworthy or disqualified in some way because of things you've done in your past or ways you have failed, go to these verses and remind yourself who you are and whose you are. He forgives you so that you can forgive yourself. This is one of the most powerful things you can do. Read every verse and memorize those that speak to you with truth and power about your standing in the family of God.

- I am God's child (John 1:12). *Having believed in Jesus as God, He accepts me as His child.*

- I am Christ's friend (John 15:15). *He calls me His friend and He is willing to reveal His plans to me.*

- I have been justified (Romans 5:1). *I have been declared righteous through my faith in Christ's death on the Cross.*

- I am united with the Lord, and I am one spirit with Him (1 Corinthians 6:7). *I have been bonded to Christ in a spiritual union, which is indissoluble.*

- I have been bought with a price (1 Corinthians 6:20). *I have been purchased at very great cost to God, so God sees me as valuable.*

- I belong to God (1 Corinthians 6:19, 20). *God claims ownership over me so that He can set me free to live abundantly.*

- I am a member of Christ's body (1 Corinthians 12:27). *God has incorporated me into the mystical body of Christ presently operative on earth.*

- I am a saint (Ephesians 1:1). *Because of my trust in Christ, God sees me as holy and set apart for Him.*

- I have been adopted as God's child (Ephesians 1:5). *I have been brought into the place of full privilege in God's family.*

- I have direct access to God through the Holy Spirit (Ephesians 2:18). *I can pray and know that my prayers get through because of the Holy Spirit.*

- I have been redeemed and forgiven of all my sins (Colossians 1:14). *I have been bought out of the slave market of sin and released from the ultimate penalty of my sins.*

- I am complete in Christ (Colossians 2:10). *I have all I need because I need Christ. He and I are a perfectly sufficient unit.*

- I am free forever from condemnation (Romans 8:1, 2). *God does not condemn me anymore because of my embrace of Christ.*

- I am assured that all things work together for good (Romans 8:28). *God is so powerful and brings good out of all the evil that comes into my life.*

- I am free from any condemning charges against me (Romans 8:31). *The Devil cannot bring an accusation against me that God will listen to.*

- I cannot be separated from the love of God (Romans 8:35). *Nothing can separate me from the love of God that is Christ Jesus... NOTHING.*

- I have been established, anointed, and sealed by God (2 Corinthians 1:21, 22). *God has planted me firmly to grow in Him. He has specially blessed me and marked me for heaven.*

- I am hidden with Christ in God (Colossians 3:3). *My real life is hidden with Christ, and all I really am in Christ will be fully displayed when Christ returns.*

- I am confident the good work that God has begun in me will be perfected (Philippians 1:6). *God has begun the process to make me like Christ, and He will not stop.*

- I am a citizen of heaven (Philippians 3:20). *My true home is in heaven with Christ. I am out of place down here.*

- I was not given a spirit of fear but of power, love, and a sound mind (2 Timothy 1:7). God has given me His Spirit to strengthen my spirit and give me new abilities.

- I can find grace and mercy in time of need (Hebrews 4:16). *Every time I need God's power, His favor, His forgiveness, and encouragement, it is mine in Christ through prayer.*

- I am born of God and the Evil One cannot touch me (1 John 5:18). *God gave birth to a new creature when I trusted Christ, and the Devil cannot touch that new creation.*

- I am the salt and light of the earth (Matthew 5:13, 14). *God has called me to help preserve what is right and good in this world, as well as to show the glory of Christ and how life should really be lived.*

- I am a branch of the true vine, a channel of His life (John 15:1, 5). *God has connected me to His inexhaustible storehouse of energy, creativity, and power. All I have to do is stay plugged in to God, and all I need for any assignment will be available to me.*

- I have been chosen and appointed to bear fruit (John 15:16). *God chose me to be one of His children. I did not get in by mistake. He wants me to show the fruit of the Spirit in my life.*

- I am a personal witness of Christ (Acts 1:8). *God has empowered me to tell others what Christ has done for me.*

- I am God's temple (1 Corinthians 6:19). *God has established His eternal presence in my body.*

- I am a minister of reconciliation for God (2 Corinthians 5:17). *I have been asked by God to tell others that He is not holding their sins against them because Christ died for all their sins. They must accept Christ's payment.*

- I am God's co-worker (1 Corinthians 3:9; 2 Corinthians 6:1). *God has been willing to work with me to accomplish His will. He has, in some sense, restricted a part of His will to my cooperation. I am working with God.*

- I am seated with Christ in the heavenly realm (Ephesians 2:6). *In terms of my position, Christ says that I carry the same authority that He has as the one seated at the right hand of the Father, the highest position of authority in the universe. Every other being is under that authority, including the Devil.*

- I am God's workmanship (Ephesians 2:10). *God is working on me to bring me to completion and will not stop until He is completely satisfied and ready to enjoy eternity with me in heaven.*

- I may approach God with freedom and confidence (Ephesians 3:12). *My ability to approach God is not dependent on my perfection but on Christ's finished work on the cross. I have freedom and confidence in Christ to come to God.*

- I can do all things through Christ who strengthens me (Philippians 4:13). *There is not one job that God will ever give me where He has not also supplied all the power I need to complete that job.*

APPENDIX 5:

THE RADICAL POWER OF FORGIVENESS

Below are some various Scriptures that are a part of a healthy forgiveness process. Read each verse and have a discussion with God about how to do these in your life. It is the discussion with God and your acting on Scripture that produces the great prayer life with God. Enjoy!

- Matthew 6:14, 15

- 1 Timothy 1:5, 19; 4:2; 1 Peter 3:16; 1 John 3:21

- Luke 23:34; Acts 16:35–40; Matthew 18:15–18; Colossians 3:13; Acts 6:1–3

- Romans 12:17–21

- Psalm 109:4–11

- Matthew 18:15

- Matthew 18

- Romans 6

- Luke 23:34

APPENDIX 5: THE RADICAL POWER OF FORGIVENESS

- Romans 8:28, 29
- Matthew 5:3–12
- Matthew 6:23–24
- Luke 17:3; Matthew 18:15–18
- 1 Peter 2:23; Matthew 19:21–35; 1 Corinthians 3:12-15; 2 Corinthians 5:10
- Matthew 5:38–42
- Matthew 5:44
- 1 Peter 2:19–25

ABOUT GIL STIEGLITZ

D R. GIL STIEGLITZ IS AN AUTHOR, SPEAKER, CATALYST, PROFESSOR, PASTOR, COUNSELOR, and leadership consultant. He speaks to thousands of people every year about building healthy and successful relationships. Gil currently serves as Discipleship Pastor at Bayside Church, a dynamic multi-site church on the north side of Sacramento, CA. He served for five years as Executive Pastor of Adventure Christian Church in Roseville, CA. He is an adjunct professor at Western Seminary (Sacramento Campus), a church consultant for Thriving Churches International, and Founder and President of Principles To Live By, a discipleship and publishing non-profit dedicated to equipping people, pastors, and churches to live out God's best for them. He has served on the board of a number of non-profit groups to help start churches, revitalize pastors, and rescue minors from sex trafficking and exploitation. He has been a denominational executive for thirteen years with the Evangelical Church of America and was the senior pastor at a mid-sized church in Southern California for seventeen years. Gil has a heart for helping people become all that God wants them to be. He believes that a "Great Life Is Great Relationships." To learn more about Gil, his books, resources, and speaking and consulting opportunities, visit www.ptlb.com.

MORE RESOURCES FROM PRINCIPLES TO LIVE BY

Books

Becoming a Godly Husband
Becoming Courageous
Breakfast with Solomon, Volumes 1 - 3
Breaking Satanic Bondage
Deep Happiness: Eight Secrets
Delighting in God
Delighting in Jesus
Developing a Christian Worldview
God's Radical Plan for Wives
God's Radical Plan for Wives Companion Bible Study
Going Deep in Prayer: Forty Days of In-Depth Prayer
Keeping Visitors
Leading a Thriving Ministry
Marital Intelligence
Mission Possible: Winning the Battle over Temptation
Proverbs: Devotional Commentary, Volumes 1 - 2
Satan and the Origin of Evil
Secrets of God's Armor
Spiritual Disciplines of a C.H.R.I.S.T.I.A.N.
The Gift of Seeing Angels and Demons: A Handbook for
    Discerners of Spirits
The Keys to Grapeness—Growing a Spirit-led Life
The Schemes of Satan
They Laughed When I Wrote Another Book about Prayer,
    Then They Read It
Touching the Face of God: Forty Days of Adoring God

Uniquely You: A Faith-Driven Journey to Your True Identity and Water-Walking, Giant-Slaying, History-Making Destiny
Weapons of Righteousness Study Guides
Why There Has to Be a Hell

Online Video Courses

Mission Possible: Winning the Battle over Temptation
Becoming a Godly Husband
The Keys to Grapeness—Growing a Spirit-led Life

Audio Files

Becoming a Godly Parent
Becoming a Godly Husband
Biblical Meditation: Keys of Transformation
Deep Happiness: Eight Secrets
Everyday Spiritual Warfare Series
God's Guide to Handling Money
Marital Intelligence: Battling for Your Marriage
Intensive Spiritual Warfare Series
Spiritual War Surrounding Money
The Four Keys to a Great Family
The Ten Commandments
Raising Your Leadership Level: Double Your Impact
Spiritual Warfare: Using the Weapons of God to Win Spiritual Battles
Weapons of Righteousness Series

www.PTLB.com

CPSIA information can be obtained
at www.ICGtesting.com
Printed in the USA
FSHW011652171019
63064FS

9 780996 885553